This book will change your o1
for the better. Drinking deeply
the truth about the harm that
employees. This book is both li
Sir 1
(

CW01501473

This is a much-needed book. Tabbin challenges the alcohol-centric culture that still prevails in many workplaces and points out what a high price we are paying, both economically and in human terms. There is a deep irony that businesses encourage their employees to drink, in the interests of bonding and building relationships, but when, as is inevitable with an addictive substance, some of those employees become addicted to it, they are shunned. The western world is facing something of a crisis in mental health, and alcohol is a contributory factor in this. I completely agree with Tabbin when she calls for alcohol awareness to be included in Wellbeing and Stress Management programmes and for those who become addicted to alcohol to be treated with compassion and not stigmatized. The sooner we can stop Alcohol Use Disorder being a taboo subject in the workplace, the better for all of us. I urge you to read this book, and assess and change your own corporate culture, so that your business and your employees can thrive.

Annie Grace, founder of This Naked Mind, and author of 'This Naked Mind – Control Alcohol – find freedom, discover happiness and change your life' and 'The Alcohol Experiment' and co-author (with William Porter) of 'This Naked Mind – Nicotine – the proven science-based method to quit smoking and vaping'

Tabbin Almond provides a thought-provoking and practical guide that will be relevant to anyone who is an employer or employed. It sets out a long overdue agenda for change to a culture that I have personally witnessed throughout my working career. From my time at medical school through to international conferences, or even dinners in the Palace of Westminster, the content of this book sadly resonates with behaviour for which I have not only been a willing participant but also regrettably a cheer leader. This did not end well for me. I now count myself now among a rising tide of people who, like the author, feel that we urgently need more recognition of the problems that alcohol can cause and compassion for those who, through no fault of their own, have developed issues with controlling their consumption. A good starting point is the workplace.

Professor Charles Knowles, Queen Mary University of London, author of 'Why We Drink Too Much'

Comprehensively researched and engagingly written, Tabbin cuts to the heart of the economic and moral arguments for why many employers should re-evaluate their alcohol cultures. The blend of personal stories, expert analysis, and depth of evidence provides a useful toolkit for companies that want to improve workplace productivity while supporting the health of their employees.

Dr Katherine Severi, Chief Executive, Institute of Alcohol Studies

Working as a consultant psychiatrist and psychotherapist in the NHS has left me in no doubt about the devastating consequences of alcohol dependence on the lives of patients and their families. Tabbin Almond's book *Bottling Up Trouble* is compelling and essential reading for all employers with an interest in the productivity and wellbeing of their workforce. Its publication comes not a moment too soon given the 32.8% increase in alcohol-related deaths since the Covid pandemic. In her punchy readable style, drawing on her personal and professional experience Tabbin takes the reader on a journey through the causes and consequences of dependent alcohol use, its impact on productivity at work, the working culture that promotes drinking and stigmatizes the drinker culminating in a Charter for Change detailing how employers can embed help with problem drinking in the wellbeing programmes in their organization. I can only congratulate Tabbin for this courageous, authoritative, and important contribution, tackling an issue of national importance.

Dr C. Susan Mizen, Consultant Psychiatrist in Psychotherapy

Bottling Up Trouble is an important book that shines a light on an issue rarely discussed. For years, many aspects of the media industry have glorified alcohol consumption as a way of social bonding, stress release, of celebrating or team building. In itself, and in moderation, this should not be an issue. However, when it is coupled with pressure to be involved or a badge of honour to have done in excess, it can become a problem.

My career has been in media research and therefore not in the heart of the agency/client world but even as a senior practitioner I still felt the social anxiety of leaving evening events early, felt the social exclusion of not being privy to the drunken antics of the night before, or part of the gang as clearly hung-over colleagues took to the podium the next morning. However, the key issue that this book exposes is the cost of this culture when things go wrong.

Whilst there is a fond acceptance of alcohol fuelled high jinks, when it tips into a regular habit and then an addiction, it is a different matter. In these situations, the mood changes and it is more the individual's character that comes into question – their ability to cope, the standards of their work their suitability as an ambassador for the company. Whilst I am sure that many companies will have their own corporate support and wellbeing policies, and many will provide comprehensive health insurance, I have seen little evidence of industry or corporate responsibility. Which leads me back to the importance of this book for not only providing a clear and pragmatic strategy for how individuals and companies can help get through this situation, but also, and equally importantly, how they can put things in place to avoid them happening in the first place. This involves a cultural change that cannot take place over night.

The good news is that the substantial research undertaken in this field for the younger generation of workers – especially the Gen Zs – indicates that younger people are drinking less since the pandemic and, more importantly, that they feel no judgement from their peers when not drinking. It seems that there is a combination of factors for this – ranging from financial (they simply can't afford it), to greater awareness of the impact on mental health (particularly in a post-pandemic world), to the fear of their behaviour being recorded and played back on social media. The research suggests that they increasingly associate being drunk with feelings of vulnerability and anxiety. Whilst this gives us grounds for hope, it should not allow for complacency. Tabbin's book is a must read for all corporations who need to understand the potential harm of any culture that glorifies alcohol to achieve their own goals, whilst stigmatizes those who fall at a wayside.

Liz Landy, Global CEO, Audience Measurement, Ipsos

As a young journalist, I considered that booze (much of it free) was part of the job. This thought-provoking book has opened my eyes to the downside of the laissez-faire attitude to all this free alcohol. Tabbin draws attention to the many ways in which the boozy culture of workplaces is harming society. It will strike a chord with the growing number of people who are questioning the role of alcohol in society, and it provides practical advice on how we can improve things.

Mike Carter, author of three books, including the best-selling 'One Man and His Bike', and freelance journalist writing for The Guardian, The Observer and the Financial Times, among others

Bottling Up Trouble is refreshingly optimistic. It doesn't just push at an open door but smashes through it. Anyone running a business or sports team should embrace it. It provides a roadmap to reframe beliefs to everyone's benefit.

Jeremy Cowdrey, Vice President, Kent County Cricket Club

This is such an interesting and thought-provoking read. Tabbin highlights the way that alcohol has had a free pass in society and how good it would be if we could change that.

Sue Cleaver, Coronation Street actor and Loose Women presenter

This book is impactful because it's written from someone who has experienced the issues that are described and has walked the path that you may be facing. Or that you want a colleague to consider.

Everyone in a business has a role to play in ensuring that their colleagues thrive. For management that's not in a controlling or mandatory way but in a sensitive and thoughtful approach that recognizes that work is life and life is work. We spend so much of our time at work – sometimes not even in a physical sense but quite often it's on our mind – that we need to acknowledge that we have a partnership with people. We can't address all the issues our colleagues face, but we can support and enable them to handle them.

There is evidence that younger generations are turning away from alcohol. That doesn't mean that in a few years there will be no more issues around alcohol consumption. There will always be a situation where alcohol isn't a part of someone's life, it has become their life. Even if the numbers are eventually much smaller, we still have a role to play in enabling people with an issue around alcohol to come to terms with their situation and playing our role in the recovery. As managers, as colleagues, as fellow human beings, we have a role to play in ensuring that people thrive.

In the interim, let's look at the role that alcohol plays in the ways that we work – do you go to the pub after work to celebrate success? This isn't just an issue for people with issues around alcohol, it's an issue for anyone with caring duties or whose belief system doesn't include alcohol. Or for people who find crowds and noise difficult (or in my case, just want to be able to sit down!). So, let's rethink ways that we make people feel that they belong. One that doesn't require a drink to make you relax – because you should already feel comfortable. As businesses, let's use the power of our people to make a way of work that helps them thrive.

Kathryn Jacob, Chief Executive, Pearl & Dean

Bottling Up Trouble is a much-needed wake-up call for corporate culture right now. Tabbin, with her compelling personal journey from advertising powerhouse to highly sought-after sobriety coach, brings a raw and insightful examination of alcohol's hidden toll on businesses. Her book doesn't just shed light on the issue – it offers practical, stigma-shattering strategies for creating a healthier, more inclusive, and ultimately more successful workplace. A must-read for any leader serious about nurturing wellbeing and boosting performance in their organization.

Christy Osborne, Sobriety Coach, author of 'Love Life Sober:
A 40-day alcohol fast to rediscover your joy, improve
your health and renew your mind'

Bottling Up Trouble is long overdue! It tackles the way alcohol on so many levels is undermining personal and organizational health and productivity, as well as the way that for many organizations it is often seen as 'rite of passage' and even progression in some cases. Organizations have allowed it to become part of their fabric; its consumption is touted as the elixir of life whilst its destructive power on multiple levels is overlooked. As a senior police officer who barely drank any alcohol when I joined the service, to have become a routine, regular, and heavy drinker by my mid 40s for just about every reason, including as a coping mechanism for stress, I have witnessed first-hand its unhelpful role within organizational culture but also its influence on countless lives whether as victims of violent crime or simply people losing livelihoods and their dignity as they spiralled into alcohol-dependant lifestyles. My own wakeup call began in 2018 but it was only when I suffered from burnout that I finally called time and subsequently have worked hard to try and change organizational culture in policing with regards to this.

Tabbin's treatment of the subject in this book is incredibly insightful. It is well thought out, factual, and helpful. It will equip organizations to rethink, re-evaluate, and reorientate but also will help to create space for healthy conversations, de-stigmatizing where necessary and supporting individuals to be their best and to better optimize health and wellbeing, alleviating stress and improving personal resilience. Organizations really can change their culture and narrative concerning alcohol and there is no time like the present to do this! *Bottling Up Trouble* will help you to uncork your organizational potential in an unprecedented way.

Retired Chief Superintendent Maria Fox,
(served in Derbyshire constabulary, West Midlands Police,
and Greater Manchester Police)

Reading sections of this book has given some great insight into alcohol, performance, and team culture. Times change, and so culture changes along with it, books like this may help shed some light to anyone that is curious as to what that change may look like and why it may be necessary.

Don Armand, Business owner and former
Exeter Chiefs and England rugby player

A much needed, insightful resource on a critical, often overlooked topic. If leaders read this book and take it to heart, they will be able to create healthier and more effective organizations, and help employees have healthier lives.

Tara Mohr, author of 'Playing Big' and founder of the
global Playing Big leadership programme for women, and
expert on women's leadership and well-being

Tabbin highlights the damage that is done when organizations encourage the use of alcohol to facilitate team bonding – damage to the business and to the individuals who work for it. And she outlines practical steps to accelerate the rate of change towards a better and more inclusive culture.

William Porter, author of 'Alcohol Explained'
and 'Alcohol Explained 2'

Bottling Up Trouble

How alcohol is harming your business
and what to do about it

Tabbin Almond

First published in Great Britain by Practical Inspiration Publishing, 2024

© Tabbin Almond, 2024

The moral rights of the author have been asserted

ISBN   978-1-78860-594-6   (hardback)
          978-1-78860-595-3   (paperback)
          978-1-78860-597-7   (epub)
          978-1-78860-596-0   (mobi)

Every effort has been made to trace copyright holders and to obtain their permission for the use of copyright material. The publisher apologizes for any errors or omissions and would be grateful if notified of any corrections that should be incorporated in future reprints or editions of this book.

Want to bulk-buy copies of this book for your team and colleagues? We can customize the content and co-brand *Bottling Up Trouble* to suit your business's needs.

Please email info@practicalinspiration.com for more details.

Practical Inspiration Publishing

MIX
Paper | Supporting responsible forestry
FSC FSC® C013604
www.fsc.org

Dedicated to my children Lucy and Eddie.

I love you both unconditionally.

Contents

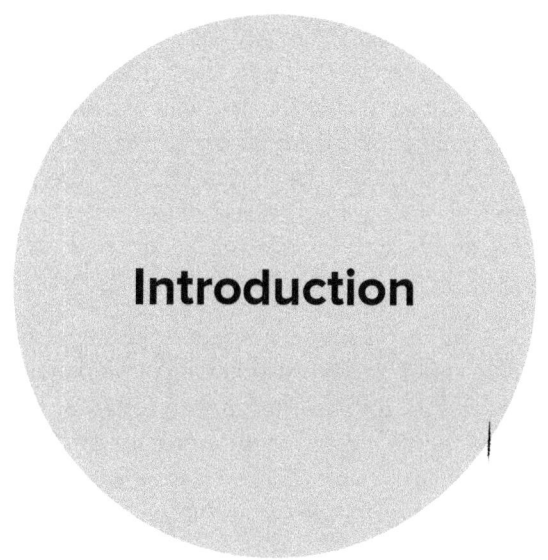

Introduction

What this book is about?

This book is about why and how you as an employer should take a long hard look at the alcohol culture of your organization. Alcohol adversely affects the productivity and profitability of many businesses, and it is also causing a great deal of human misery. Both of those should bother you. Whatever your sector, productivity matters. And so should being a decent human being, and looking after the people you work with. And as I'm sure you know, these two factors are inextricably linked – happy employees are more productive.

Alcohol plays a significant role in Western culture. Yet the mental health issue of Alcohol Use Disorder (AUD) carries such a stigma that it is hardly ever talked about. Mental health per se is no longer a taboo subject, and this is definitely a shift in the right direction. Many businesses and organizations now offer wellbeing programmes, and this, too, is a really good thing.

But it is very rare for alcohol and AUD to form part of the wellbeing conversation, and that needs to change.

Wellbeing programmes cover stress management but make little or no reference to alcohol, and this is a serious oversight. It's the elephant in the room. Drinking alcohol is a very significant contributor to poor mental health as I will explain in this book. In a nutshell, many people drink alcohol in the belief that it will help them to relax and de-stress. But in fact, the reverse happens. Drinking alcohol leads to the release of adrenalin and cortisol, making stress and anxiety worse, not better. And, to quote the wonderful Michael Caine, 'not a lot of people know that'.

In this book, I will explain why an understanding of alcohol and AUD should be baked into every wellbeing programme. I will help you to understand the impact of alcohol on your own organization and how to assess the alcohol culture of your own organization using my Bottling Up Trouble (BUT) assessment tool. I will suggest ways in which you can change the culture.

By destigmatizing alcohol addiction, you can create a culture shift that leads to employees feeling safe enough to ask you for help, and for you to be confident that you are offering the right kind of help. For that to happen, you need to see the commercial benefit in changing the culture, and to have a clear roadmap for achieving this. So, I will address both of these issues in some detail.

I want to emphasize that this is absolutely *not* a business-bashing book. But it *is* the book that I wish my bosses had read when I was starting my working life.

Nor should this be seen as an anti-alcohol book. Although I have chosen to live an alcohol-free life, I am not seeking to convert everyone to my way of thinking. But I *do* want to encourage you to ask serious questions about the role of alcohol in the workplace culture.

If alcohol was invented today, governments around the world would rush to make it illegal. But it *does* exist and is widely used.

Indeed, it is promoted extensively and in Western cultures, we are positively encouraged to drink it. But it is addictive. And addiction to alcohol (alcoholism, AUD, call it what you will) is a source of shame and stigma.

Why now?

My focus in this book is on alcohol and the workplace; for many of us, our drinking 'career' either began or accelerated at work. When someone starts drinking, they do so in the belief that it will help them have fun, bond with others, and unwind. But drinking to unwind can and does lead to problems. I am writing this in 2024, and there is no doubt that the last few years have been very stressful, with the pandemic, working from home, isolation, political instability, and a cost-of-living crisis. Where there is stress there, too, will be self-medication with alcohol.

Stress and alcohol

Here in the UK, alcohol-specific deaths have risen sharply since 2019, increasing by 32.8% from 2019 to 2022 (up from 7,565 in 2019 to 10,048 in 2022).[1] And alcohol-related deaths are at a record high since records began to be collected in this way in 2001. This big increase is against a backdrop of very stable figures for the period from 2001–2019; the ONS statistician James Tucker commented:

> Alcohol-specific deaths have risen sharply since the onset of the coronavirus (COVID-19) pandemic, with alcoholic liver disease the leading cause of these deaths. This rise is likely to be the result of increased alcohol consumption during the pandemic. Research has suggested that people who were already drinking at higher levels before the pandemic were the most likely to have increased their consumption during this period.

---

[1] Source: Office for National Statistics.

It is worth noting that alcohol-specific deaths are only the tip of the iceberg. These are the deaths which are wholly attributable to alcohol. The majority of these (some 75%) are caused by alcoholic liver disease, with mental and behavioural disorders due to alcohol accounting for a further 12%, and accidental poisoning by, and exposure to, alcohol causing a further 6%. Data suggests that alcohol-specific causes account for roughly a third of all deaths that can actually be attributed to alcohol. According to the rather grandly named Office for Health Improvement and Disparities, there were 20,970 deaths related to alcohol in England alone in 2021. That is a lot of lives cut short. The same source estimates the potential years of life lost due to alcohol-related conditions, and suggests that in 2020, this figure was just short of 300,000 for men in England, and 138,000 for women. Worryingly, the figure for women shows a marked upward trajectory.

And I should point out that most people get ill and need hospital treatment before they die. In 2021–2022, there were 948,000 admissions to hospital for alcohol-related conditions in England alone.[2] This results in a huge burden on the public purse.

The reasons why people drink are complex, but the data clearly show that the stress and isolation of the pandemic led to an increase in drinking. Sadly, we will see this play out in increased mortality rates for many years to come.

In this book I will explain why alcohol can only ever make stress worse. I will also explain the nature of alcohol addiction, and how damaging it is for businesses and organizations.

I firmly believe that now is a good time to be addressing this challenge. The pandemic changed things, for the worse. In England, average household expenditure on alcohol increased by 23.8%[3] during 2020. We have emerged from the pandemic with more people than ever struggling with addiction to alcohol, and more people than ever working from home, at least part of the time. We know that some of them are feeling isolated and

---

[2] Source: Public Health England.
[3] Source: NHS Digital – statistics on public health, 2020 versus 2019.

disconnected and, unfortunately, these are ideal circumstances for addiction to take hold.

Grounds for optimism

The data from the past few years are worrying, but there are also reasons to be optimistic, with numerous signs that the tide is changing.

- Sales of low/no alcohol brands are up:
  - Market analysts Mintel report that the value of sales of low/no alcohol drinks has more than doubled in the six years to 2018–2023, and they project that they will increase by a further 80–100% over the next five years.

- Moderation is becoming a thing, particularly with the young:
  - Mintel also report a growth in the proportion of UK adults who say that they are consciously moderating their alcohol intake in comparison to what they would usually drink (up from 33% in 2019 to 38% in 2023).
  - The data show that younger adults are more likely to have cut back than those who are older: 46% of 25–34-year-olds report that they have reduced or limited their alcohol intake, and 18–24 years olds are the most likely to be teetotal (33% versus 22% for the general population).

- There is some understanding of alcohol's effect on the emotional wellbeing of those who drink it:
  - 35% of alcohol drinkers worry about its effect on their emotional wellbeing, rising to 53% amongst 18–34-year-olds. And these concerns are reflected in their behaviours, with 66% of alcohol drinkers who are concerned about alcohol's effect on their emotional wellbeing choosing to drink no or low alcohol drinks.

- An increasing proportion of the young do not drink alcohol at all:
  - NHS England data estimates that 42% of young women aged 16–24 either do not drink alcohol at all or have not done so in the last 12 months. This figure has doubled in 11 years, and although the absolute figures are slightly lower, we see a similar trend with young men.

The dilemma that society is facing

I suspect that the majority of readers of this book will feel somewhat conflicted. There will be feelings of hypocrisy, reading about, and recognizing, the 'evils' of something that they enjoy. It may feel like a case of 'do what I say' not 'do what I do'. And that's ok. As a society, we are in a real mess when it comes to alcohol. The message to people seems to be 'you must drink this addictive substance in order to fit in but, whatever you do, don't get addicted to it or you will find yourself ostracized'.

Don't worry about it, this is not a 'you' problem, it is much bigger than that. The hypocrisy is happening at a national and international level. Governments around the world *know* that alcohol is addictive. They know that the addiction is seriously detrimental to their country's economic and social wellbeing, yet they seem to have a very poor understanding of how addiction works, and consequently have no effective measures in place to help those who become addicted. Governments are not blameless. They happily take the excise duty on the sale of alcohol, and we are talking significant sums of money – the Office for Budget Responsibility's provisional figure for excise revenue from alcohol for 2023–2024 for the UK is £12.6 billion. I believe this means that governments should shoulder some of the responsibility when people become addicted to it. At the very least, they should ensure that they are providing accurate education to prevent addiction and plentiful high-quality support for those who need it. But neither of these things is happening.

Table 0.1: Definition of a unit/standard drink, and recommended safe drinking limits by country

Country	Definition of a unit/ standard drink	Number of units in common drinks	Recommended safe limits		Source
			Men	Women	
USA	14.0 grams (0.6 ounces) of pure alcohol	Beer – 12 ounces or 341ml – 5% alcohol content = 1 unit	2 drinks per day, i.e.: 14 drinks per week	1 drink per day, i.e.: 7 drinks per week	Center for Disease Control
		Wine – 5 ounces or 142ml – 12% alcohol content = 1 unit			
		Spirits – 1.5 ounces or 43ml – 40% alcohol content = 1 unit			
Canada	13.45 grams of pure alcohol	As for USA	2 standard drinks per week		Canadian Center on Substance Use & Addiction
Australia	10 grams of pure alcohol	Beer – small glass 9285ml), 4.8% is 1.1 standard drinks	10 standard drinks per week, and no more than 4 in one day		Australian Govt. Department of Health & Aged Care
		Wine – 150ml, 13.5%, is 1.6 standard drinks			
		Spirits – 30ml, 40%, is one standard drink			

New Zealand	10 grams of pure alcohol	As for Australia	3 drinks per day and at least 2 days with no drinking – max of 15 standard drinks per week	2 drinks per day and at least 2 days with no drinking – max of 10 standard drinks per week	New Zealand Ministry for Health
United Kingdom	8 grams of pure alcohol	Beer – ½ pint of 'regular' strength beer is 1 unit	No more than 14 units per week. If drinking close to 14 units per week, these should be spread across 3+ days, and with at least 2 alcohol free days per week		Dept of Health & Social Care
		Wine – 12% ABV – standard glass (175ml) is 2.1 units			
		Spirits – single measure of 25ml = 1 unit			

Education on the harm caused by alcohol is poor to non-existent. The World Health Organization published a statement in *The Lancet Public Health* in January 2023: 'when it comes to alcohol consumption, there is no safe amount that does not affect health'. But Canada is, at the time of writing, the only country to have revised their recommended safe drinking guidelines. In Table 0.1, I list the recommended safe drinking guidelines for different countries – you can see how they vary – there isn't even universal agreement on what constitutes a unit of alcohol, with a unit in the UK being 8 grams of pure alcohol, and a unit in the USA being not far off double at 14 grams.

No wonder people are confused and tend to ignore the guidelines! It feels as though the advice is being made up randomly. Or rather, that decisions about setting guidelines are influenced by factors other than those related to public health. Government policies around the world are inevitably very short term, as politicians are interested in staying in power after the next election. This means that there is little or no incentive to take decisions which are unpopular in the short term and for which benefits will only accrue slowly over the medium to long term, even if those benefits are significant. Short termism and chasing the popular vote rarely make for good decision making.

Perhaps things are clearer when it comes to getting people the help they need when they find that they are no longer in control of their drinking? Well, unfortunately not. The most common form of 'treatment' is based around Alcoholics Anonymous (AA) and the 12-step programme. This can be delivered entirely by the voluntary sector (in the form of AA meetings), through private rehab clinics, or occasionally in state-run clinics. Now I really don't want to knock AA or the 12-step programme – the method has worked effectively for millions of people and has saved countless lives. But it is not the only option, and it doesn't work for everyone. I tried it but had a number of issues which I cover in Chapter 6. And as I will explain, the AA approach is contributing to the shame and stigma that causes people to hide the extent of their problem rather than get the help that they need.

My back story

You may be wondering about my background and what makes me qualified to write this book. So let me share my story. It's not a tale of a spectacular rock-bottom, but of a slow slide into an unhappy dependence. It is the sort of story I hear every day from my clients.

I grew up in a family where alcohol featured large. My parents both drank a fair bit, and so did friends and family. If you came to our house any time after about 5pm, you were highly unlikely to be offered a cup of tea. Instead, you'd have been offered some of my parents' (infamously disgusting) home-brewed beer, or 'something stronger'. Drinking was normal and by the time I was 16, I was going to the pub regularly with friends, where my drink of choice was Cinzano and lemonade – this was long before the WKDs of this world had been invented, but served much the same purpose, a sweet concoction that got you tipsy pretty quickly. By the time I got to university, I was an enthusiastic social drinker, and a year in Cognac as part of my degree course certainly fuelled that enthusiasm. So, I was perfectly set up to start my career in the boozy advertising industry of the 1980s.

I started out in the media department and would be out to lunch with media owners almost every day of the week and then to the pub with colleagues most evenings. This was followed by partying hard at the weekends. And if I was at home in the evening, I would generally have a few glasses of wine, and tell myself that I was very sophisticated. The years went by, I was doing reasonably well at work, got married and had two children. And as I found it easy to forego alcohol during my pregnancies, I reassured myself that I couldn't possibly have a problem with booze. But I was aware that I drank a bit differently to other people, and I had a number of blackouts.

We left London and moved to Devon (home for me), and my husband worked abroad a lot, and I got into the habit of drinking alone. And when he was home, I'd drink even more, and I started hiding how much I was drinking. By my mid-40s, I knew in my heart of hearts that I had a problem. I tried Alcoholics Anonymous, but it never clicked for me. I came away from every meeting feeling that I wasn't 'bad' enough to be there, that I hadn't reached a low enough rock bottom to call myself an alcoholic. So, I floundered on alone, waking up in the mornings feeling dreadful and vowing not to drink that day, but with the first of many glasses of wine in my hand as I prepared supper that evening. Rinse and repeat.

I remember telling my husband that I felt that I was sleep-walking through life, and that I felt alcohol had something to do with my low mood and lack of presence. I read Alan Carr's book, *The Easy Way to Control Alcohol*, and signed up for a day of hypnotherapy to address my problem with alcohol. And that worked for several years, and I remained alcohol free through a very turbulent time – the break-up of our marriage, big financial problems, and a breast cancer diagnosis. But being told that the cancer had spread to all of the lymph nodes they tested was very scary, and my response was to turn to my trusty so-called friend, the wine bottle. I had more surgery, followed by that delightful combo of chemo and radiotherapy, during which time I didn't drink much at all. But once I had recovered, and was back at work, the drinking ramped up again. I was living alone and drinking alone. And I was back in that awful rinse and repeat cycle, full of self-loathing for my lack of willpower.

One day I googled 'Am I an alcoholic?' and came across an organization called *This Naked Mind*. I ordered the book of the same name, by Annie Grace, and it made so much sense. Here was an approach which didn't characterize me as a weak-willed alcoholic and didn't blame me. Instead, I learned that this was not my fault, and that if I could identify and reframe the reasons why I liked to drink, I would lose the desire to drink. And that is exactly what happened. I signed up to do a three-month online course and was very quickly alcohol-free and have been so ever since.

I feel that it is important to share my story. Anyone who is struggling with alcohol can gain some comfort from the fact that someone else has overcome their addiction. And by the way, there is no merit in the 'my rock bottom was lower than your rock bottom' thinking. This is an addictive substance. Annie Grace uses the analogy of a runaway train that is headed for a steep gorge with a broken bridge. Unless you get off that train, the outcome is inevitable. And nitpicking about when to get off that train is to miss the point entirely. It's about getting off it whilst you still can.

Another reason that it is important to share my story is that it means I am practising what I preach. I firmly believe that there is nothing shameful about developing an addiction to alcohol, so it behoves me to share my story openly. I am 100% not ashamed. I will share my story far and wide, and the only details I omit are those that might cause discomfort to others. If you want to read a longer version, see my website.[4] The reality is that my dependence on alcohol developed, not because I am flawed, or have a defective character, but simply because I'm a human being. I had a (fairly long) period of being addicted to a substance that is addictive to all human beings who drink enough of it. Where is the shame in that? And whether you, as a reader, think you might have a problem yourself, or you lead a team of people, one or more of whom may

---

[4] www.winetowatercoaching.com/my-story

have a problem, I would urge you to apply the same thinking to yourself and/or to your team members. This is nothing to be ashamed of. *There should be no stigma attached to being addicted to alcohol*, and I see it as my calling to reduce and ultimately eradicate the shame and stigma that exists around alcohol addiction. If I can at least see progress in this area before I depart this earth, I'll die a happy woman.

This Naked Mind

So, what was it that made *This Naked Mind* work for me when other methods didn't? And why do I feel so strongly that this method should be made available to anyone who needs it?

1. I learned that there was nothing wrong with me. I wasn't genetically flawed or lacking willpower. This was not my fault.
2. The logical conclusion from point 1, above, is that there should be no shame or stigma attached to developing AUD.
3. Once we remove the shame and stigma, people will be much happier to ask for help with their AUD, in the same way as is now happening with mental health concerns. Problems will be dealt with at a much earlier stage, thus minimizing so much unhappiness.
4. Willpower is not a successful strategy for overcoming AUD. And when it fails, people will be left feeling diminished and hopeless.
5. For the foreseeable future, society and our culture will encourage us to drink alcohol – we need to empower people to make better decisions.
6. Other methods stop with the behaviour change – what matters is that you stop drinking, even though it may be a real struggle and you may be miserable. (AA even has a term for this – the 'dry drunk' – which is used to describe the person who is sober but still yearning for a drink.)
7. *This Naked Mind's* focus is on helping people change their thoughts and beliefs about alcohol so that they no longer want to drink. These beliefs are generally around

alcohol's role in relieving stress, celebrating, having fun, overcoming shyness, fitting in, and many more. And once the desire to drink has gone, it is pretty easy not to do it.

8. As I will demonstrate in Chapter 11, *This Naked Mind's* methodology is both successful and cost-effective.

Terminology

This book is about the harm that alcohol does to organizations and individuals, and there are a lot of different terms used to describe what we are talking about. There is the horribly loaded 'alcoholism', the marginally less loaded alcohol addiction, or alcohol dependence. But all of them imply a degree of disempowerment. The term that is increasingly used in medical circles is Alcohol Use Disorder or AUD (see the Appendix for the definition). This is the term that I will use throughout this book, and it is important to understand that AUD is a spectrum disorder, ranging from mild to severe.

I like AUD as a term because it doesn't skate over the fact that a substantial proportion of people in the Western world use alcohol. What we are talking about is what happens when that use gets out of hand, when it gets 'disordered'. And the other reason I like it is that it feels far less pejorative than the other terms. *Alcohol Use Disorder is something that can happen to anyone who ever drinks alcohol, and it is unhelpful and unkind to use terms that imply blame or trigger shame.*

One final point to make is that this book is specifically about alcohol and its impact on businesses and organizations. However, drugs are also a problem, both prescription drugs and illegal drugs. I do not cover them for three reasons:

1. Drugs are outside my area of expertise.
2. There is already reasonably good help available, in most countries, for those who develop an addiction to prescription drugs.
3. It is difficult for employers to in any way 'sanction' the taking of illegal drugs – actively supporting those who become addicted to illegal drugs could be seen as sanctioning illegal behaviour.

PART 1

How alcohol is holding your business back

1

The financial costs to organizations of the absenteeism and presenteeism associated with alcohol

I realize that the only way I am going to convince you to change the culture of your organization is to demonstrate that to do so will benefit your organization. And that is quite a challenge, because I'm trying to prove a hypothetical. So far, we haven't seen significant changes in workplace attitudes to alcohol, so it is hard to make comparisons. And then there is the fact that the stigma around alcoholism is such that people are deterred from 'admitting' that the reason they are off sick is due to excessive alcohol consumption. This means it is very likely that there is significant under-reporting of the impact of alcohol, with many cases categorized as mental health issues such as stress, anxiety, and depression. Even so, there is plenty of evidence to support my arguments, and I'm going to start with the all-important commercial impacts of alcohol consumption before discussing its human impact.

There are two ways in which alcohol consumption impacts the financial health of your organization. The first relates to the drinking habits of your employees and the drinking habits of their immediate families, and how these impact that employee's performance and productivity. The second is about how alcohol consumption impacts the wider economy.

The wider economic impact

Let's look at the wider economy first. As I set about digging into the research on this, I was struck by how out of date the figures were for both the UK and the USA. I am not the only one to have noticed this, and here in the UK, the Institute of Alcohol Studies (IAS) is one of many groups to have called for the data to be updated. So far, the UK government has not done anything about this.

Way back in 2003, a Cabinet Office Strategy Unit report was published, surveying the evidence on the cost of alcohol to society. This put the 'external' cost to society in England and Wales at £21 billion – this is the costs imposed by drinkers upon others and excludes any personal impact. At today's prices, this equates to £35 billion.

Another study,[5] by the National Social Marketing Centre took a broader view in their study in 2006–2007, and estimated that the total social cost of alcohol in England alone was £60 billion, which equates to £87.5 billion at 2023 prices. The breakdown of this figure is shown in Table 1.1.

Those are big numbers. But perhaps the UK is an anomaly? Well, no. Data from the USA's Centre for Disease Control (CDC) estimates that excessive alcohol consumption cost the country US$249 billion in 2010[6] – these data do not appear to get updated in the USA either. That works out at US$2.05 per drink, or US$807 per person. And they estimate that 72% of the total cost is accounted for by lost productivity in the workplace, which works out at US$179 billion. According to the Bureau of Labor Statistics, there were 160 million people working in the country in 2010. This means that the cost per employee of lost productivity due to alcohol was a staggeringly high US$1,119 per year.

---

[5] The costs of alcohol to society, briefing, October 2020.

[6] www.cdc.gov/alcohol/data-stats.htm

Table 1.1: National Social Marketing Centre – estimates of total social cost of alcohol, 2006–2007

Details of cost – England only (not whole UK)	Cost in 2006–2007	Cost at 2023 prices
Cost to individuals and households, including crime and violence, private health and care costs, informal care costs for families, lost income due to unemployment and spending on alcohol above guideline levels	£22.6 billion	£33 billion
Human values costs: the pain and grief associated with illness, disability, and death	£21.9 billion	£31.9 billion
Costs to public health and care services	£3.2 billion	£4.7 billion
Costs to other public services such as social care, criminal justice, and fire services	£5.0 billion	£7.29 billion
Costs to employers due to lost productivity, absenteeism, and accidents	£7.3 billion	£10.6 billion
Total	£60 billion	£87.5 billion

North of the border, they seem to update their figures rather more frequently. The Canadian Substance Use and Harms study estimates that alcohol cost their economy CAN$19.7 billion in 2020, with lost productivity being the greatest contributor to this (c.46%), followed by healthcare costs (28%), criminal justice (20%), and other direct costs (6%). They also estimate that the annual per person costs of alcohol increased 21.3%, from CAN$427 to CAN$518 between 2007 and 2020. And that figure of CAN$518 per person for alcohol compares to CAN$63 for cannabis, CAN$80 for stimulants excluding cocaine, CAN$186 for opioids, and CAN$293 for tobacco.

What alcohol is costing individual businesses

I'd now like to drill down a little more into the productivity data and what alcohol is costing businesses.

Absenteeism

The UK's Health and Safety Executive (HSE) estimate that between 3–5% of all absence from work is due to alcohol consumption. But this is an old estimate, which precedes the pandemic, and we know that the lockdowns led to an escalation in drinking. There was a significant increase in deaths from alcohol-specific causes, mainly liver disease, in the UK (9,641 in 2021, up by 27.4% since 2019), and it is logical to expect that there will also have been an increase in absence from work due to alcohol-related sickness. So rather than 3–5% of all absence from work being due to alcohol consumption, we can realistically increase the figure by at least 25% – so we are looking at 4–5% of all absence from work being down to alcohol. That might not sound too bad, but there are some other factors to be taken into consideration:

1. Heavy drinking (the type that is likely to lead to health issues and absence from work) is more prevalent amongst those who are in work than amongst those who are unemployed or not working.[7] This probably has something to do with affordability, and it does rather dispel the myth that 'alcoholics' are down-and-outs who are living on the streets.

---

[7] ONS – adult drinking habits in Great Britain 2017 (dataset has been discontinued).

2. The heaviest drinking occurs amongst those in professional and managerial roles, i.e., those who are in more senior roles (where they are exerting influence over others). These people are the most expensive to employ, and the most valuable to the organization, which increases the loss to the business if they are off sick or below par due to alcohol.

The nature of the stigma around AUD means that people are highly unlikely to tell their employer that they are off sick due to drinking too much alcohol, so we do have to use informed estimates, backed up by statistics on things like hospital admissions due to alcohol. But let's start with the estimates of the cost of alcohol to employers:

- The Chartered institute for Personnel and Development conducted a study in 2007, called 'Managing Drug and Alcohol Misuse at Work'. This study is now out of date, but unfortunately it doesn't appear to have been repeated... there seems to be a pattern here with so much out-of-date data. The 2007 study found that 40% of employers mentioned alcohol as a significant cause of low productivity. The pandemic is likely to have pushed that figure up, and not down.

- Another study conducted by the HSE (*Don't mix it – a guide for employers on alcohol at work*) estimated that between 3–5% of all absence from work is due to alcohol consumption. According to the Office for National Statistics, the average annual number of days lost to sickness, per worker, was 5.7 in 2022. On the basis of an eight-hour working day, that equates to each worker being off sick for 45.6 hours every year, of which an average of around two hours are accounted for by alcohol consumption. It doesn't sound a lot until you think that this is an average. Many people don't drink at all, and it is only the minority where their drinking will lead to them having to take time off work to recover.

I am afraid that this next section makes rather gloomy reading. Let's look at the number of deaths each year from alcohol-specific causes. Figure 1.1 below shows how this has been gradually increasing over the past 20 years, with a very significant increase attributable to Covid. In 2021, there were nearly 10,000 deaths directly attributable to alcohol in the UK. This represented an increase of 7.4% on the previous year and was a staggering 27.4% higher than for 2019 (pre-pandemic).

Figure 1.1: Alcohol-specific deaths registered in the UK

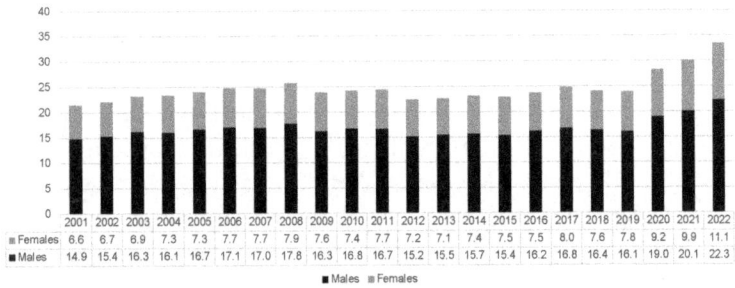

Source: Office for National Statistics, 2022

Presentee-ism

Presentee-ism is the term used to describe people being at work, but either hungover or still intoxicated. And as you can imagine, it is a fiendishly difficult thing to quantify. There is no test you can conduct to assess if someone is hungover – the alcohol may have left the bloodstream but (as anyone who has ever had a hangover knows only too well), the effects last a lot longer.

There are actually two ways that presentee-ism impacts an employer:

1. The cumulative, long-term effect on individuals who are heavy drinkers (which will, in time, lead to increased rates of absence due to sickness, and potentially to their leaving the workforce and/or their death). This is of course tragic for the individuals concerned and undoubtedly has a ripple-effect around the organization. The way that it is

communicated clearly needs to reflect the individual's right to privacy, but this can lead to the dreaded rumour-mill going into overdrive, and this in itself can be damaging to the organization.

2. The short-term impact of someone being at work drunk or hungover. This was the subject of a study called 'Financial Headache',[8] conducted by the Institute of Alcohol Studies (IAS) in the UK in 2019.

The 'Financial Headache' report is an excellent piece of research conducted amongst a sample of 3,400 British workers, and weighted to the working population. The IAS conducted the study because they felt that this form of presentee-ism was a significant drag on the economy, which needed to be quantified. And the findings make really interesting reading – and pretty alarming reading if you are leading a business.

The research asked people if they had ever been to work either hungover or under the influence, and if they had done so in the past six months. The findings were that 42% of respondents had gone to work hungover or intoxicated at least once, and 9% had done so in the previous six months. This figure of 9% is actually lower than previous studies, but the difference may be explained by different methodologies. We can also hypothesize that this pre-pandemic figure is likely to be higher now.

But let's stick with this figure of 9% of workers having gone to work hungover or intoxicated on at least one occasion in the last six months. What impact did this have on their effectiveness at work, and therefore on the overall productivity of the organization that employs them? Assessing an individual's productivity is hugely subjective, and all sorts of biases can creep in. There is probably no perfect method, but the one used by the IAS in this study seems suitable to me. They asked the respondents to rate their own performance on a normal day, and then when impaired through alcohol. The second question was worded thus: 'Please rate how well you performed your job

---

[8] Institute of Alcohol Studies, *Financial Headache – the cost of workplace hangovers and intoxication to the UK economy.*

on the days you went to work even though you were hungover or under the influence of alcohol.'

On average, workers rated their own performance as 39% less effective than normal when they were hungover or drunk. From this the researchers were able to calculate the cost to the economy. And it works out at £1.4 billion a year. The researchers do point out that there were two respondents who reported that they were either hungover of intoxicated virtually every day, and whilst this is actually typical of studies of this type, and does appear to reflect reality, they were concerned that they might be inflating the scale of the problem. So, the research team excluded the data from these two potential outliers, and re-calculated the total economic cost. It dropped to £1.2 billion a year, so the true figure is somewhere between £1.2 billion and £1.4 billion a year. Every year. For the UK alone (see Figure 1.2).

Figure 1.2: Formula for calculating the economic cost of alcohol-related presentee-ism

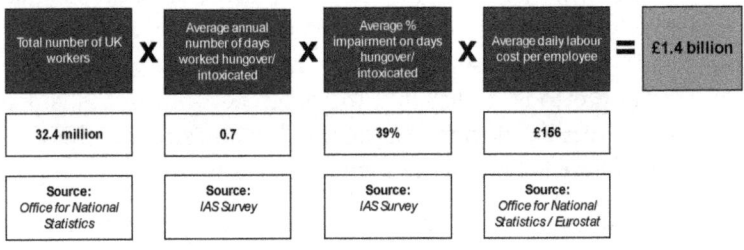

Source: IAS Financial Headache Study, March 2019. Sample 3,400 British workers. Reproduced with their permission

Another factor that we need to consider is that this study is focused on the employee who has been drinking. It does not quantify *the effect on co-workers* of an employee showing up at work hungover or under the influence. But they were able to ascertain that there is an effect, and that the employee who has been drinking will typically under estimate the impact that this has on those they work with. Only 7% of respondents believe that their behaviour had an effect on their team's effectiveness, but those in the team see things differently, with 28% of them believing it had adversely affected their productivity. And of course, this impacts team morale too, with 18% of colleagues believing that there was a negative effect on team morale, whilst only 7% of respondents believed this to be true (see Figure 1.3). So, an employee with AUD is having a seriously negative impact on the productivity and mental wellbeing of those around them.

Figure 1.3: Impact of respondent's/colleague's working whilst hungover or intoxicated

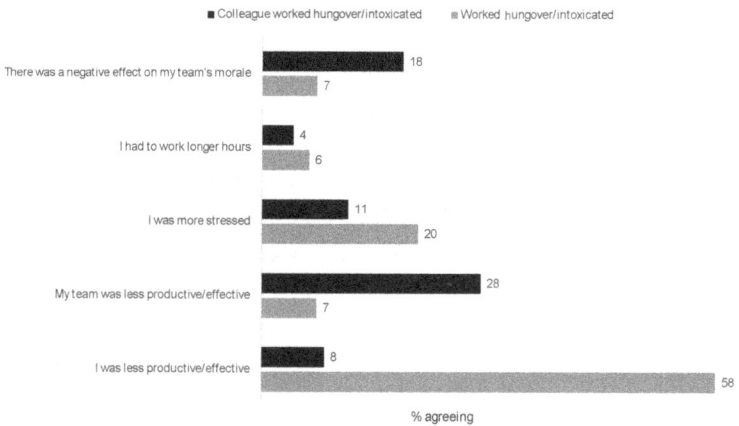

Source: IAS Financial Headache Study, March 2019. Sample 3,400 British workers. Reproduced with their permission

As a slight aside, it is also interesting to note that one in five respondents reported that being at work hungover or under the influence was a source of stress for them. We'll look in more detail later at the relationship between alcohol and stress, but for now, just observe the irony that the substance we drink to unwind and relieve stress seems to be making it worse.

Of course, the figures I have quoted above are the headlines and they mask some significant variations, particularly by industry. Perhaps unsurprisingly, the problem is greatest in the hospitality industry, where 52% of respondents have been to work intoxicated or hungover (versus an average of 42%) and 16% had done so in the last six months (versus an average of 9%). Other 'high risk' industries were retail and construction. The sectors with the lowest prevalence of workers being hungover or intoxicated were health and social care, and education, but even so, 30% had done so at least once. There are a number of recent studies showing that the pandemic led to increased rates of drinking in the medical profession and this will almost inevitably have led to an increase in the proportion of them going to work suffering from the after-effects of drinking.

Employers probably want to know who, amongst their workforce, is most likely to turn up intoxicated or hungover – that is, who the high-risk groups are. The data show that they are likely to be male, full-time workers who are high earners – the highest earning group (£60k and above) are more likely than any other income group to have done this in the last six months (13% versus an average of 9%). The data also show that those on the lowest income are significantly less likely than average to have done this at least once but not in the last six months (22% versus a 42% average), and to have done so in the last six months (7% versus a 9% average). In terms of age, we see that 35–44-year-olds are the most likely to have been to work drunk or hungover, but it is those who are younger than this who are the most likely to have done so in the past six months. This suggests that this may be a pattern of behaviour that some people 'grow out of' and/or that the behaviour is becoming less widespread across the board. There is evidence to support both hypotheses, and, encouragingly, there is increasingly strong evidence that the young (<24) are less likely to drink alcohol/to drink excessively than previous cohorts of this age.

So, to sum up on the short-term costs of presentee-ism. We see that 9% of British workers show up for work hungover or intoxicated at least once in six months, and that when this happens they are 39% less effective than normal. The IAS estimates that this costs the UK economy between £1.2 and £1.4 billion a year.

The loyalty factor

I was off sick for nearly a year when I had breast cancer. At the time I worked for a Devon-based advertising agency, Bray Leino. They deserve a name check because they treated me absolutely brilliantly. They knew that I had been going through some personal challenges (financial and marital – I won't go into the gory details but we are talking Challenges with a capital C). They had already helped me by paying for me to see a brilliant therapist for a few months. That arrangement had come to an end before my cancer diagnosis, but as soon as I told them the news, their response was:

1. Don't worry about money. We will continue to pay you as normal and you can just do what work you can when you feel up to it.
2. Go back to the therapist if it would help, and we will pick up the bill.

That was ten years ago, and I still get emotional when I think about how extraordinarily well they looked after me. The senior management and HR teams were incredible. But so were my colleagues. Everyone was amazingly kind. A few days after my first chemo session, I felt fine and decided to go into the office. It turned out I wasn't fine. I sat at my desk, feeling more and more nauseous. Fearing that I might not make it to the loo, I just ran down some steps and outside, and proceeded to throw up all over Gordon the gardener's gorgeous lawn, in full view of colleagues who were having a meeting. In no time, they were at my side with a chair, some water and some paper towels... and a lot of hugs.

Towards the end of my chemo, the agency ran a competition with a prize of tickets to see a fabulous exhibition at the Tate (Matisse's Cut-Outs), plus travel and accommodation for two in London. I can't remember exactly what the brief was, but it involved writing a short piece and my submission was about choosing my attitude. I made reference to a brilliant and inspiring book by Debra Veal, called *Rowing It Alone*. Debra and her then-husband gave up their jobs and put all their life savings into buying a boat and taking part in the Ward Evans Transatlantic Rowing Challenge. But less than two weeks in, her husband, who was by far the more experienced oarsman of the two of them, was unable to carry on. He discovered that he suffered from severe agoraphobia. The open sea terrified him. They duly radioed for help, and the rescue crew (and her husband) were taken aback when Debra refused to get on the helicopter, saying that she was going to carry on alone. It was a really tough challenge for a couple. Even tougher for someone on their own. What I loved about this book was her mantra and the three letters she painted right in her eye-line when she was rowing: C Y A which stood for Choose Your Attitude. And every morning, she would decide what her attitude was going to be that day – Accepting? Grateful? Determined? Brave? Patient? – I adopted this way of thinking during my cancer treatment, and it certainly helped me. And I was so thrilled when the Chief Exec sent an all-staff email saying I had won the prize, and shared what I had written. I was even more thrilled when I received lots of emails from colleagues saying how well deserved this was.

Now the reason I have shared all of this detail about how my employer treated me when I was ill is because it made me incredibly loyal to them. I would never have left to go to another advertising agency, nor to take up a client-side role (which would have been a more likely option as there aren't many good advertising agencies in rural Devon). The only reason I left was because I had discovered (somewhat late in life I admit) that I had a calling. Once I had overcome my own addiction to alcohol, I felt compelled to help others and to spend the rest of my working life changing the culture and reducing the stigma and shame of alcohol addiction. Once I was certified as a coach, I cut back from five days a week to four, and spent about 18 months coaching one day a week and at weekends and in the evening. But it wasn't enough. So, I resigned to do it full time. I knew it was the right thing to do, but even so, I handed in my resignation letter with a heavy heart. These people had been so good to me, and I felt bad about leaving. Their reaction was, predictably, wonderful. Hugs, tears, and lots of congratulations and good wishes.

They treated me amazingly when I was diagnosed with something that attracts no shame or blame, and my loyalty to them was huge. Imagine how off-the-scale-loyal someone would be if they were treated the same way when they were suffering from something that does (albeit wrongly) attract blame and shame. Imagine how much better it would be for you to retain the member of staff who has a problem with alcohol and help them overcome it.

The cost of firing and hiring

There are a lot of hidden costs to dismissing someone, especially for something like alcoholism. Such a dismissal inevitably leads to gossip and conjecture, and in my experience, there is a loss of productivity when someone leaves under a cloud. How serious and how long-lived that is will depend on how effectively you, as part of the leadership team, communicate what has happened and why. Any dismissal will take up time for senior management and HR teams, who will be concerned about the threat of a claim for wrongful dismissal. If it goes to a tribunal, or worse still, to court, the consequences can be really serious, both financially and in the damage it does to the morale of everyone else in the organization. Even if the company comes out on top, a legal claim can still lead to negative publicity and serious reputational damage. I'm sure you can imagine the negative headlines that could arise: 'Stressed and overworked executive driven to addiction.'

We also need to consider the issues around recruiting a replacement. First, it can be very expensive, with recruitment agencies typically charging 20–30% of starting salary. According to the ONS, the average full-time salary in the UK in 2021 was just over £38,000, so the average recruitment agency fee is in the order of £9,500. And there are the hidden costs, like the time spent writing job descriptions and briefing recruiters. And it can take a long time to find the right person, and get them in post, particularly if they are for a senior or very skilled role and with a long notice period. It can easily take six months or longer to have a new person in post, and even then, it will take them a while to be as productive as the person they have replaced. The cost to the business may not end there – Talent Insight Group also point out that 57% of all hires made in the last 12 months weren't working out well in some capacity, and 25% were not working out at all. Retention of staff is not just a 'nice-to-have'. It makes very good business sense.

I would argue strongly that dismissal of anyone with AUD should not be a knee-jerk reaction. There is a better way, and that is to support the individual and help them to overcome their problems. The loyalty that an employer can gain from this, from the employee and the wider workforce, can be considerable. And it is also important to point out that giving people a fair chance is the right thing to do morally as well as commercially.

Alcohol awareness should be included in wellbeing programmes

Establishing a reputation as an employer who genuinely cares about the wellbeing of its employees can be very beneficial to your employer brand. Imagine how attractive it would be to join a company knowing that *whatever* mental health issues you might face during your time with them, you would be treated with dignity and compassion and not vilified or fired. (And yes, I do see AUD as a mental health issue, and so should all employers.)

You may already be spending significant time and money developing wellbeing programmes, and the management of stress and anxiety is a core part of that. What I am calling for is for those programmes to address the fact that alcohol can only ever make those problems worse and not better. Programmes should help people recognize signs that they may be developing a problem with alcohol and offer clear signposting of where to go to get help. Most of all, wellbeing programmes should reassure people that for this employer, AUD is seen as a mental health issue and not a disciplinary issue.

A caring approach to mental health pays dividends

It may sound a bit nebulous to claim that being seen as an employer who cares will help you to recruit and retain good staff, but it really isn't. According to Deloitte's 2023 Gen Z and Millennials Survey, eight in ten of these two demographic groups cite mental health support and policies as a top factor when considering an employer.

When I was talking to employers about their wellbeing programmes, as part of my research for this book, I came across a degree of frustration about low rates of take-up of the help that is being provided. And the Deloitte research backs this up – take-up *is* indeed low, as shown in Table 1.2.

Table 1.2: Rates of take-up of mental health resources by Gen Z and Millennials

Mental health support tool offered	Gen Z offered and used	Gen Z offered and not used	Millennials offered and used	Millennials offered and not used
	%	%	%	%
Resources to help reduce stress	30	29	26	27
Access to mental health apps/digital services	25	29	22	25
Paid-for counselling/ therapy	23	28	19	26

Source: Deloitte 2023, Gen Z and Millennials Survey

It is easy to imagine that these low take-up rates could lead to the decision to provide such help being called into question. But that would be a mistake. The evidence is crystal clear that the help is needed. In total, 46% of Gen Z and 39% of Millennials claim that they are stressed and anxious most or all of the time, and this is driven mainly by work pressures. They clearly need help. And with the help that is being provided, things *are* improving, slowly. Over half of these younger employees acknowledge that their employers are taking mental health seriously and that this is resulting in positive change, and these figures represent an increase on the previous year. However, the resources remain underused. The Deloitte report puts this down to the stigma around mental health:

> Many employees would not feel comfortable speaking openly with their manager about stress or anxiety. And among the 39% of Gen Zs and 34% of Millennials who

have taken time off for mental health, more than half did not tell their employers the real reason for their absence... the continued hesitancy to discuss the reasons for mental health related absences or to use mental health resources is likely due to a persistent mental health stigma in the workplace.

Deloitte have identified the stigma around mental health in general being a barrier to employees taking up the help that is on offer. How much worse is this stigma when it comes to alcohol addiction, which is rarely even part of the mental health conversation and for which virtually no help is provided?

There is a *lot* of work to be done in de-stigmatizing mental health issues in general and addiction in particular. People will only open up and ask for help when they feel they can do so without fear of judgement. This is a leadership issue. We need managers and leaders in organizations to talk openly about their own issues and how they have overcome stress, anxiety, and addiction. When employees witness this and can see that these 'disclosures' haven't hampered the career development of those individuals, they will start to have some trust. But until then, they will fear that they risk being branded as 'flaky'.

I hope the day will come when someone struggling with alcohol addiction feels completely safe asking their employer for help, gets the help they need and goes on to tell others how the organization helped them to overcome their problem. Imagine what a positive impact that would have on them and their families, their colleagues, their employer, and on wider society.

Chapter summary

There are a number of ways in which alcohol can be a financial burden to your business:

- A drag on the national economy – in the order of £80m per year for England alone, at 2023 prices (note: For England only, not the UK).

- Absenteeism – conservative estimates suggest that c. 5% of all absenteeism is due to alcohol. The reality is likely to be *much* higher than this, as stigma means that employees who are absent because of a hangover will generally claim to be suffering from something else.

- Presenteeism – estimated to cost £1.4bn per year in the UK alone, and this figure does not include the impact on co-workers of someone being intoxicated or hungover at work.

- There are a number of costs involved if you need to dismiss a member of staff because of an alcohol problem – disruption, threat of legal action, reputational damage, cost of hiring, training and embedding a replacement. It is far better to help that individual overcome their problem, for which they are likely to reward you with a high degree of loyalty.

- An employer with a reputation for genuinely caring about staff wellbeing will be able to attract and retain the best people. Employer attitudes to mental wellbeing are a particular focus for Gen Z and Millennials.

2

The human cost of alcohol

Inclusivity

One of my fellow coaches, Wendy, used to be a lawyer, and she was expected to attend corporate functions to 'wine and dine' clients. She and her husband were really keen to start a family, but Wendy suffered repeated miscarriages. She was naturally avoiding alcohol, and the doctors were advising her to avoid stress too (both tricky for a corporate lawyer). Whether she was in the early stages of a pregnancy, or recovering physically and mentally from a recent miscarriage, or just hoping to get pregnant again, she didn't want to drink. She told me that she is sure she would have received support from her co-workers if she had told them what she was going through, but quite understandably, she didn't want to discuss her fertility with anyone other than her husband and her doctor. So, she 'pretended', attending function after function either nursing a glass of wine without actually drinking any of it, or making up reasons why she wasn't drinking. She felt she had to have an excuse. She felt she couldn't just say 'I'll have a soft drink, please' without it becoming an issue. This is an example of someone feeling excluded and uncomfortable because they don't want to drink, and it is something we *must* change.

Why, oh why, are we so bothered about the chemical formula of what someone chooses to put in their glass and in their body? It is their business, and theirs alone.

There are so many different circumstances which may lead to someone preferring a non-alcoholic drink. This is not an exhaustive list, and I'm sure you will be able to add to it:

- Anyone who just wants to feel healthy and well (physically, mentally, and emotionally).
- Anyone who knows they may need to drive or operate machinery.
- Women wanting to get pregnant.
- Women in the early stages of pregnancy (usually the first trimester up to 12 weeks, after which most people 'announce' their pregnancy).
- Men who understand that the chances of he and his partner conceiving a healthy baby are enhanced if he abstains from alcohol.
- Anyone who feels they could be taken advantage of or sexually exploited if they get drunk.
- Anyone who is looking after someone who might need their help in the middle of the night (young child, elderly relative, or someone disabled).
- Anyone taking certain medications.
- Anyone suffering from depression, anxiety, or stress (all of which are made worse by alcohol).
- Anyone who has been advised by their doctor to take a break from alcohol.
- Anyone who already has any degree of liver damage.
- Anyone concerned about their health (see the next section for more information on the health risks of drinking).
- Anyone who is grieving – it is much easier to process raw emotions without alcohol muddying the picture.
- Certain ethnic and/or religious groups.
- Anyone who wants to perform well, physically or mentally, the following day.
- Anyone who has problems with their sleep.

Most of the reasons in this list are personal, and there should be no compulsion to share them with anyone, and particularly not with colleagues. So, it follows that there should always be acceptable non-alcoholic alternatives on offer, and that what someone decides to drink should never be an issue.

Pressure to drink to fit in

But it goes much deeper than this. The alcohol culture in many organizations means that, even though it may theoretically be possible to stick to alcohol-free drinks, the individual who doesn't drink will be made to feel like an outsider.

I'll give you an extreme example. Imagine you are a top-class rugby player. Your team wins a notable victory away in France, and you played a significant part in that victory, playing one of the best games of your entire career and scoring a last-minute try to seal an unlikely victory. According to the press, you have been 'playing out of (your) skin' this season. What you and very few others know is that there is a reason why you have been playing so much better... you have been alcohol-free for several months now. And so far, you've managed to hide it from your teammates. But tonight, there is a big celebration, and tradition and the culture of the club dictates that you drink a pint of red wine, downing it in one. Damned if you do (horrible hangover next day, don't play well for a couple of weeks and upset your partner who liked you so much better now that you have stopped drinking). Damned if you don't (made to feel you are not one of the team, ridiculed, have your stamina questioned, given a spurious fine for 'behaviour unbecoming to a team member' and asked to explain yourself).

I would love to say that this could never happen. Surely a professional sportsperson wouldn't feel pressurized into drinking. Well, yes, it happens all the time. The England and Wales Cricket Board (ECB) published a report in in 2023, entitled 'Holding up a Mirror to Cricket', in which they said 'drinking, as part of a post-match routine or team bonding, has been, and continues to be a consistent feature of cricket, *at all levels*' (added emphasis). And they observed that there was clear evidence that drinking was often seen as a necessary part of 'fitting in'. This is a particular problem in a game where so many participants are from ethnic minority groups who do not drink alcohol. The report says 'at club level, there is still a drinking culture so Muslim players are never integrated that well. (There is) peer pressure on young players to join in with the drinking as they don't feel part of the team otherwise. Most social events are centred around alcohol.'

The same report also highlighted some completely unacceptable alcohol-fuelled behaviour, particularly around the conduct and attitudes of men towards women. This is putting women and girls off playing the game. One parent of a young girl is quoted in the report as saying 'pissed guys "sexting" my daughter. It's demeaning and threatening, so she stopped playing to avoid being exposed to that crap. How is this even allowed to happen in 2021?' Former England cricket captain Andrew 'Freddie' Flintoff is fondly thought of as a 'good lad' for his drunken antics involving a pedalo,[9] but the reality is that he bitterly regretted the incident which cost him the vice-captaincy for the rest of that tour in 2007. Interestingly, he has not drunk alcohol for over a decade, and said recently 'one of the reasons I stopped drinking is that I am prone to suffer from depression. Drinking doesn't help one bit. I don't touch it now.'

And the picture is really grim when we look at what goes on in amateur sport. University initiation rites are truly shocking and so extreme that they have resulted in deaths as was the case with a young student by the name of Ed Farmer,[10] who was in his first year at Newcastle University. This is far from a unique story, but I think it sticks in my mind because of his name – my son is called Ed, and my father was a farmer. Anyway, the unfortunate Ed Farmer went on an Agriculture Society night out which involved various initiation rites including drinking multiple triple vodkas in a very short space of time. During the course of the evening, he collapsed and had to be carried through a Metro station. Someone also shaved his head. By the time someone realized that he was in serious trouble, it was too late. He had suffered a cardiac arrest and, tragically, died in hospital. Sadly, there are people like Ed who die every year, and it is not just those who die who we should be worried about. The initiation rites culture will have contributed to the normalization of heavy drinking for many young people, and this in turn will have led to countless people becoming addicted.

---

[9] www.radiotimes.com/tv/sport/cricket/freddie-flintoff-reveals-the-real-reason-for-his-drunken-pedalo-trip/

[10] www.theguardian.com/uk-news/2018/oct/22/newcastle-student-died-after-initiation-bar-crawl-inquest-told

These extreme examples can serve as cautionary tales, but less extreme examples are going on all around us, in all sorts of workplace environments, and we just accept it as part and parcel of working life. When I started work in advertising in the 1980s, every board director had a fridge in their office, and those fridges were kept well-stocked with alcohol. I couldn't tell you if there was anything non-alcoholic in them because at the time, that would not have interested me. But I checked with a friend who was PA to the Media Director, and she told me that there was one Director she was aware of who liked his fridge to be stocked with Clamato which he drank without vodka. But for everyone else, the only non-alcoholic drinks in those fridges were mixers. This was a long time ago, and alcohol-free beers and spirits weren't really a thing back then, but sparkling water was... it just wasn't stocked in those fridges. The amount of drinking represented in the TV series Mad Men was not an exaggeration.

Things have, mercifully, changed a bit since those days. It is no longer the norm for directors to have booze-stocked fridges in their offices, nor for there to be a free bar every Thursday night. But it is still extremely common for (unofficial) team-bonding sessions to be held at the local pub, often with a manager putting their credit card behind the bar. These evenings are great ways for junior members of the team to get to know their superiors and to build relationships with them. The employee who either doesn't want to go or who literally can't go due to family or other commitments is made to feel somewhat left out, both at the time and again the following morning when people are recounting 'funny' stories from the night before. 'You had to be there' takes on a special poignancy in these circumstances, particularly when unconscious bias kicks in and those who are considered for promotion are those who are regular attendees at after-work drinks and therefore seen to be 'team players'.

The lack of inclusivity can be hard to spot, but it is there, and you as a responsible employer may already be taking steps to rethink your strategies for bringing the workforce together. There are numerous ways this can be achieved which I will cover later on. For now, it is enough to recognize that exclusion is almost definitely going on in your organization. And that reducing or eradicating it would make you a much more attractive employer. And you'll have a happier, healthier, and more productive workforce as a result.

The health risks of drinking alcohol

Alcohol is a poison. We all know that, don't we? Why else do we get hangovers and throw up if we have too much of it?

As employers, we are aware that drunk employees are a liability and hungover ones are thoroughly unproductive. Yet many organizations either encourage some drinking, or at least turn a blind eye to it, until it becomes overtly problematic for the business.

But for the employee, the consequences of excessive or dependent drinking can extend far beyond the risk to their job. The health risks of drinking are considerable, so much so that the World Health Organization (WHO) has stated that the safe level of alcohol consumption is zero. They state that alcohol is a causal factor in over 200 diseases, health conditions, and injuries. Below I list some of the main ones.

Cancer: The WHO cite alcohol as a group 1 human carcinogen, causally linked to the following types of cancer:

- mouth and throat (oesophagus);
- larynx (voice-box);
- colon and rectum;
- liver;
- breast (in women).

Additionally, there is evidence that drinking more than three alcoholic drinks a day increases the risk of pancreatic, stomach, and prostate cancer.

As a woman who has had breast cancer and been fortunate enough to survive it, I have been particularly interested to research the statistics behind alcohol and breast cancer. I found that the research consistently shows that drinking alcohol increases a woman's risk of hormone-receptor-positive breast cancer. It can increase levels of oestrogen and other hormones associated with hormone-receptor-positive breast cancer. And it may also increase breast cancer risk by damaging DNA in cells. The charity breastcancer.org says:

> Compared to women who don't drink at all, women who have three alcoholic drinks per week have a 15% higher risk of breast cancer. Experts estimate that the risk of breast cancer goes up by another 10% for each additional drink women regularly have each day.

So, by this measure, a woman who is drinking a relatively modest two glasses of wine a day is more than twice as likely as her teetotal peers to go on to develop breast cancer.

It is also known that girls aged 9–15 who drink between 3–5 units of alcohol a week have three times the risk of developing benign breast lumps, some of which will go onto to become malignant in later life.

Relatively little research has been done into the impact of alcohol on the risk of recurrence of breast cancer in women who have already had it once. But the research that has been published does show an increased risk, even at very modest levels of drinking.

These stats are pretty scary. And they are food for thought if you are an employer who is in any way facilitating female employees to drink alcohol regularly. Here in the UK, we are not a particularly litigious bunch, but I imagine that it is entirely possible in other jurisdictions that a woman who gets breast cancer might sue an employer if she felt under pressure to drink regularly in the course of her work, for example when entertaining clients.

Liver damage: This is perhaps the best-known of all the risks associated with drinking. We even use the expression 'liverish' to describe the after-effects of drinking, and this is because the liver is very much on the front line when it comes to dealing with the toxic effects of drinking. The liver breaks down alcohol into acetaldehyde, which is another toxic substance, which the liver has to then turn into harmless by-products. But it is easy to overwhelm the liver's ability to process alcohol, and this leads to damage to the liver. The main ways this happens are:

- Inflammation and alcoholic hepatitis – the alcohol irritates the liver; this leads to inflammation, and once it is pronounced, this inflammation is known as alcoholic hepatitis. It leads to the cells of the liver becoming damaged and dying. The liver is famously able to regenerate itself, but if the drinking is excessive or prolonged, the liver may not be able to regenerate fast enough to prevent disease becoming serious. This will cause symptoms such as jaundice, fatigue, abdominal pain, and liver enlargement.

- Fat accumulation – alcohol consumption can lead to the accumulation of fat in the liver, a condition known as alcoholic fatty liver disease. This is reversible if alcohol consumption is stopped, but it can progress to more severe liver diseases if alcohol abuse continues.

- Fibrosis – prolonged alcohol abuse can lead to the development of fibrous scar tissue in the liver, a process which is called fibrosis. This can impair liver function and disrupt the normal structure of the liver.

- Cirrhosis – in some cases, continued alcohol use and the progression of fibrosis can result in cirrhosis, which is a late-stage liver disease. This involves extensive scarring and damage to the liver tissue, leading to impaired liver function and potentially to liver failure.

- Liver cancer – alcohol abuse increases the risk of developing liver cancer. This occurs most commonly in individuals with alcoholic liver disease, especially in cases of cirrhosis.

Early stage alcohol-related damage to the liver is generally reversible, but it is important that it is caught early and that the individual reduces their alcohol intake, or preferably quits altogether, in order to give the liver the best chance of recovery.

Cardiovascular system: All of the following are made more likely by excessive alcohol use:

- High blood pressure (hypertension) – this is a concern because it leads to more serious conditions such as heart attacks and strokes.

- Irregular heartbeat – alcohol can cause disruption in the heart's electrical system, which can lead to irregular heart rhythms such as atrial fibrillation or other arrhythmias. And these abnormal heart rhythms can increase the risk of blood clots, strokes, and other cardiovascular complications.

- Weakened heart muscle – alcohol abuse can directly weaken the muscle of the heart, so that it contracts less effectively, and this means that its pumping capacity is impaired. And pumping oxygenated blood around the body is what the heart is there for – a damaged pump is not what we need!

- Heart attack or cardiac arrest – this is what happens when the heart suddenly stops beating effectively; as we know, this can prove fatal.

- Stroke – alcohol consumption disrupts the blood's clotting ability and contributes to the formation of blood clots, which can lead to strokes.

Immune system: Alcohol impairs the immune system in a number of ways:

- Reduces the production of immune cells and antibodies.

- Disrupts the communication between immune cells, rendering them less efficient at co–ordinating a response to infections.

- The damaged liver is less able to process and eliminate toxins.

- Causes inflammation in the gut and other tissues, contributing to immune system disfunction.

The bottom line is that heavy drinkers are much more susceptible to infections and take longer to recover from them.

Brain health:

- Alcohol disrupts the balance of the neurotransmitters, which can lead to low mood and 'brain fog'.

- Alcohol impairs the brain's ability to regulate functions like sleep and co-ordination.

- Alcohol can cause permanent structural changes in the brain, particularly in the areas responsible for memory and decision making.

- Overall cognitive function (i.e., ability to think clearly) can be permanently damaged.

We all know that our brains are sub-par when we have a hangover, but it is important to know that this can become a permanent state of affairs.

I hope that this last section has given you pause for thought – having a few drinks after work may seem like innocent fun, but if it becomes very regular or excessive, it may result in you or your employees paying a heavy price.

Alcohol's impact on mental health

Intuitively, it makes sense that happy employees are also more productive employees, and so it is reassuring to know that research confirms this. A study called 'Happiness and Productivity' conducted by Warwick University[11] demonstrated that when interventions were made to make people happier, their productivity increased by 10–12%. The same study showed that unhappy employees were 10% less productive. And Gallup's study, 'The State of the Global Workplace', has consistently shown that employees who are engaged and satisfied are more productive and have a positive impact on their company's financial performance. The same Gallup study shows that those who are least engaged are the most likely to consider leaving, with all the cost implications for you as the employer that I discussed in the previous chapter.

---

[11] Happiness and Productivity – Oswald et al.

So, it makes sound commercial sense for you to do what you can to ensure that your staff are happy and engaged. What role does alcohol play in this? Many employers labour under the misapprehension that the supply of free or subsidized alcohol and the culture of bonding over a beer is making their employees happy. But this really is a misapprehension. The happiness from drinking alcohol lasts around 20–30 minutes and is more than offset by what follows.

In Chapter 7, I will explain in detail the chemical processes that go on in the body when we drink alcohol. The top line is that after 20–30 minutes of pleasure (from dopamine), there is then a prolonged period of 3–4 hours of low mood, accompanied by feelings of stress and anxiety. So, the alcohol you are encouraging your employees to drink is leading to short-term happiness which is more than offset by longer-lasting low mood, stress, and anxiety.

Brenée Brown points out, in her book *Atlas of the Heart*, that a sense of belonging is an essential ingredient in happiness. Belonging can take many forms, from being loved and valued within our family as we are growing up, to developing strong communities socially and at work. It is very difficult for someone to give their best if they don't feel that they fit in. As a responsible employer, you will want to ensure that the organization's culture around alcohol does not make people feel excluded – it is the kind and commercially astute thing to do.

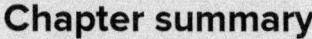

Chapter summary

- Alcohol should be considered a Diversity, Equity and Inclusion issue – it is still all too common for employees to be made to feel uncomfortable if they choose not to drink. Cultural norms of yesteryear are no longer acceptable and simply need to change.

- Drinking alcohol is associated with numerous risks to a drinker's physical health, including cancer, liver damage, cardiovascular problems, weakened immunity, impaired brain function, and brain damage.

- Alcohol is also directly associated with the most common forms of mental ill-health, in that it contributes to depression, stress, and anxiety. It is a deep irony that so many people claim to drink for relaxation and stress relief, when alcohol is actually doing the opposite and exacerbating unhappiness.

3

The reputational costs associated with alcohol

People do stupid, dangerous, violent, and even criminal things when they are drunk. This may result in them being injured, in a police cell or, in extreme cases, with them or someone else in a mortuary. And whilst these are individual tragedies, they often reflect on that individual's employer, and can damage that employer's reputation. And it is the reputational risk to you as a business that I want to look at in this chapter.

The most damaging cases are those in which the employer might be seen, however unfairly, to be responsible for the drunkenness and any harm that may result from it. These are the cases where the alcohol was either supplied by the company, or where the drinking of it was approved of, condoned, or even expected by the company culture. There have been cases where an employee has claimed that their drunken misdemeanours are not their fault, but their employer's, because their employer supplied the alcohol. This is a complex legal area and there are, of course, differences in both the law and the interpretation of the law around the world. Generally speaking, the legal position is that individuals are responsible for their own actions, but that doesn't stop people seeking to hold their employer responsible. Such cases can attract a lot of media attention. The public remember the story rather than the legal outcome, and that can be very damaging for the employer, as the auditing firm PricewaterhouseCoopers (PwC) know only too well. They were sued for alleged negligence by an employee, Michael Brockie, after he suffered a brain injury on a work night out in

2019. Staff at the Reading (UK) office were encouraged to attend an after-work 'pub golf' evening. There was considerable pressure to attend the evening and an email from one of the managers said, 'I expect absolute attendance from all of those who attended last year's invitational. Nothing short of a certified and countersigned letter by an accredited medical practitioner will suffice as excuse.' The event involved visiting nine pubs ('holes') where they would consume a specific drink. They were 'scored' on how few swigs they took to consume the drink, and these scores were recorded on cards that were printed and distributed in the office – in other words, it was all pre-planned. Brockie got so drunk that he couldn't remember anything that happened after about 10pm. He was found lying in the street with a very serious head injury that meant he had to be put into an induced coma. Half of his skull had to be removed and he was still suffering 'persistent cognitive symptoms' at the time of the claim three years after the accident. I have not been able to find the outcome of this claim, which makes me believe it was settled out of court. There can be no doubt that the media coverage of the claim was damaging to PwC's reputation.[12]

A case where 'vicarious liability' involving alcohol was proven is that of *Bellman vs Northampton Recruitment*. Clive Bellman attended a company Christmas party and stayed at a nearby hotel, on expenses. Along with several colleagues, he carried on drinking at the hotel and got into an argument with his Managing Director, Mr Major, who punched him twice, causing him to hit his head, leading to a brain injury. He successfully sued the company, saying they were vicariously liable for the assault by Mr Major.[13]

And a similar thing happened in California in the USA where the family of Dr. Jared Purton, who was killed by a drunk driver, successfully claimed against his killer's employer, the Marriott Hotel.[14] The driver was called Michael Landri and he worked as a

---

[12] www.theguardian.com/business/2022/aug/22/pwc-sued-by-employee-who-lost-half-his-skull-after-pub-golf-outing

[13] https://lawprof.co/tort/vicarious-liability-cases/bellman-v-northampton-recruitment-ltd-2018-ewca-civ-2214/

[14] https://casetext.com/case/purton-v-marriott-intl

bartender at the Marriott Del Mar Hotel. The hotel held a party in December 2009 for its employees and management, and Landri, who hadn't worked that day, arrived at the party having already drunk some beer and whiskey at home. Along with two others, he got a lift to the party, and he took a flask with him, which he refilled at least once during the party with more whiskey. By all accounts, he was visibly inebriated by the time he left at around 9pm, again getting a lift. And he didn't drink any more alcohol after leaving the party. After being at home for about 20 minutes, Landri decided to get in his car to drive one of his drunk co-workers home. During the journey, Landri crashed into a vehicle driven by Dr. Purton, killing him. He had a 0.16 blood alcohol level, which is double the permitted level of 0.8. He pleaded guilty to gross vehicular manslaughter whilst under the influence of alcohol and received a six-year prison sentence. Now, where this case gets interesting, from an employer's perspective, is that the victim's parents filed a wrongful-death action against the Marriott as well as against Landri. *They alleged that the hotel held the party for its own benefit, with the aim of improving relations between employees, between management and employees, and to increase the continuity of employment by providing a fringe benefit.* I have italicized this, for emphasis, to really draw your attention to it. Haven't many businesses supplied alcohol to employees in order to derive these benefits? It has certainly been the norm everywhere I ever worked.

Perhaps the Marriott was irresponsible, providing unlimited quantities of free alcohol to people? Well, no. They actually did what I would have recommended, or at least that was the plan. Their intention was to serve only beer and wine, and to limit this to two drinks per person by issuing tickets to be exchanged for alcohol. But that is not what happened on this occasion (nor indeed, on previous occasions). It seems to have been common practice for employees to drink strong spirits at these events, and indeed there was evidence that a Marriott manager had served strong alcohol to employees on this occasion. A hotel manager testified that 'historically there has been a lot of drinking and not a lot of control at these types of [employee] parties'. In other words, heavy drinking at these parties was part of the corporate culture. The court deemed that *Landri was acting within the scope of his employment while ingesting alcoholic beverages at the party.* The Marriott argued that their responsibility ended once the employee was safely home but the legal counterargument was that what matters is the act on which the liability is based and not *when* the act results in injury. The court argued that if the cause of the accident occurred within the scope of employment, there was no reasonable justification for cutting off an employer's potential liability as a matter of law simply because an employee reaches home. Rather, the employer's potential liability should continue until the risk that was created within the scope of the employee's employment dissipates, i.e., until he sobers up enough to drive legally.

Now, I've got to be honest, I'm not a lawyer, and it did take me a fair while to dig up these cases where the employer was deemed to be responsible for the employees' actions whilst under the influence of alcohol supplied by the employer. There don't seem to be a huge number of cases, but that doesn't necessarily mean that they don't exist. They may have been settled out of court and kept quiet. And anecdotally, that does seem to be the case. But whether they are rare or rather more common, it is incontrovertible that there are some circumstances where an employer can be held liable for the results of an employee's drinking. The circumstances in question are that the employer supplied the alcohol and/or that the corporate culture encouraged heavy drinking. And there are many industries and employers around the world for whom that is true. It therefore follows that there are a lot of employers facing the potential of serious reputational harm.

But there is a third form of reputational damage that we haven't yet touched on. I am thinking of the cases where the employer is not directly responsible for the supply of the alcohol and may not condone a heavy-drinking culture in the workplace. Even though it is not their fault, the employer can be adversely affected when an employee's drinking causes harm or offence to someone else or becomes a source of media attention. There is an expectation that you should recognize that your employee has an issue with alcohol and that you should ensure that the employee gets help and that nothing bad happens. But of course, it may be very difficult for you to spot the looming problem – alcohol dependence is still very much a taboo subject, and employees will keep it hidden rather than ask for help, meaning that you may not realize the extent of the problem until it is too late. There are several ways in which an employee's inebriation can result in damage to your reputation:

1. Social media blunders – an employee can get drunk and post inappropriate or offensive content on their social media profiles, linking it to their employer. This can quickly go viral, leading to public outrage and damage to the company's reputation.

2. Inappropriate conduct – for example, at a professional conference, an employee overindulges in alcohol during a networking event. They engage in rude or offensive behaviour, such as making inappropriate comments to fellow attendees including potential clients of business partners. This can damage the company's relationships with current and prospective clients and tarnish its reputation.

3. Drunk driving – any employee who is arrested for a drink-driving offence is likely to attract media attention, particularly if the drinking was work-related. This can really harm a company's reputation as it implies negligence in their employee management and safety policies. If the employee's role involves driving members of the public, it can be hugely damaging. Think of the huge publicity surrounding the (luckily very rare) cases of airline pilots showing up to work over the alcohol limit.

4. Client entertainment gone wrong – an employee is responsible for entertaining important clients over a dinner during which alcohol is served. During the course of the evening, the employee drinks too much and becomes belligerent or makes inappropriate advances, resulting in the client feeling uncomfortable and disrespected. This jeopardizes the client relationship and reflects poorly on you as an employer. If it includes sexual impropriety, this will obviously be damaging to the abused individual, and

can lead to very serious reputational damage to you as an employer.

5. Revealing confidential information – while attending an industry event, an employee with access to sensitive company information drinks too much and starts sharing confidential information. This is a breach of trust and can be detrimental to your business relationships and market position. It may even have legal ramifications (for example, if it leads to insider trading).

6. Public altercations – an employee becomes involved in a public altercation or a fight whilst intoxicated, and the incident is captured on video and shared on social media. The company's name may be associated with the negative behaviour, potentially harming its reputation, particularly if the video goes viral.

7. Failure to meet professional standards – in some professions, maintaining a high level of professionalism is essential. For example, if a doctor, lawyer, or teacher attends an event (work-related or not) and gets drunk and behaves inappropriately, that can damage not only their reputation, but that of their employer and of their profession as a whole.

8. Failure to meet customer expectations – in the service industry, an employee who serves customers whilst under the influence may provide a poor service, leading to customer complaints and negative reviews which reflect poorly on you as the employer.

As you read through the list above, you may have been struck, as I was, by how many examples you are aware of from your own working life, where this, or something similar, has happened. And very often there will be another form of socially unacceptable behaviour accompanying the inebriation, be it sexism, racism, class hatred, or homophobia. And of course, none of these reflect well on you as an employer either! And generally speaking, alcohol is the disinhibitor which means that these other behaviours are displayed. I would contend that drunk hate crimes are more common than sober hate crimes, and there is research that supports this.[15] And the reason why, recent research[16] has shown, is that even one alcoholic drink can make people change their judgements about what is right and wrong, meaning that they are more likely to harm other people and animals physically, and to indulge in deviant sexual behaviours or to accept bribes.

So, we have seen that, in extreme cases, you may be held legally responsible for the drunken actions of your employee, which would inevitably result in major reputational damage. However, such damage can also be caused even when you are not legally liable for the employee's inebriation. In the age of social media, such incidents can quickly get out of control.

Let me close this chapter with a couple of examples. First, the Comcast technician who attended a service appointment with a customer, at their home in Washington, USA, back in 2014. When the technician arrived, he was slurring and his movements were unsteady, so the customer suspected he had been drinking. The customer decided to record the interaction with the technician on their phone, and the video showed the man struggling to do his job, and eventually falling asleep on the customer's couch. The customer posted the video online and it quickly went viral, resulting in widespread criticism of Comcast and raising serious doubts about the quality of their service. The company had to issue a public apology but even so the story proved hard to live down.

In a more recent example, there was a tragic video that appeared on YouTube in 2023, featuring an Oklahoma teacher who was clearly drunk at school, and who was suspected of drinking in the classroom. It is a sad story of a woman who was clearly suffering from AUD and deeply unhappy. She should not have

---

[15] Study in the journal *Alcoholism: Clinical and Experimental Research*, 2013.

[16] *Alcohol and Morality: One Alcoholic Drink is Enough to Make People Declare Harm to Others and Behave Impurely*, 2023, Mariola Paruzel-Czachura, Katarzyna Pypno and Piotre Sorokowski (study not yet peer-reviewed).

been teaching whilst intoxicated, and she clearly has to accept responsibility for that. But it also reflects poorly on the school and their hiring policy. Luckily no pupils came to any harm, but the outcome could have been very different, given that she was three times over the drink-driving limit.

Chapter summary

- Bad things can and do happen when people are drunk. And whether they have been drinking in the course of their job, at an after-hours work event or in a purely private capacity, if something bad happens, this can have a serious impact on the employer's reputation as well as on that of the individual concerned. In extreme cases, and depending on the law in the country concerned, it may result in a legal case against the employer.

4

The societal factors that hold businesses back from changing their culture around alcohol

How we came to believe in alcohol's magical powers

If alcohol can be as damaging as we have seen, why is it that we believe it has such magical powers?

I'm afraid that my old profession, advertising, is at least partially responsible. I attach no blame to the agencies or the brand owners for this; they are doing nothing illegal. But they are undoubtedly fuelling a desire to drink alcohol. Great advertising makes people *want* things that they don't *need*. And there is some truly great advertising out there for alcohol.

Having spent over 35 years working for various advertising agencies, I know exactly what these brands are setting out to do. However, I signed a lot of NDAs (non-disclosure agreements) in my time, and so I need to be very careful here, and stick to generalities. So here is what alcohol ads are seeking to do.

Increase penetration

This simply means that they want to increase the proportion of the population who ever drink alcohol. Some 40 or 50 years ago, the strategists looked at the data and saw that women and young people were under-represented; this therefore represented an opportunity. Some of you may be old enough to remember Babycham, a brand which was developed to appeal to women, and particularly those who hadn't grown up in households where women drank. Babycham was a very accessible brand and part of its appeal was its apparent sophistication (with the hint of Champagne in the name). It was sold in small bottles, which helped women to keep tabs on how much they had drunk.

Many decades later, around the turn of the century the alcohol industry started to market so-called 'alco-pops', which were single unit bottles of highly palatable vodka-based drinks that tasted like sugary soft drinks but packed a punch. These were clearly designed to be entry-level or 'starter' drinks, to overcome the 'problem' that many teens really disliked their first taste of alcohol. By launching something sweet, palatable, and strong, the industry was able to get these young drinkers hooked much faster than would otherwise have been the case. The fact that many of these drinkers were under the age of 18 (the legal age for drinking alcohol in the UK) was completely unintentional of course! What a happy accident for an industry that is not known for its marketing accidents.

We have also seen the deliberate 'democratization' of wine, which had previously been something of a minefield for the uninitiated, and an area of snobbery, elitism, and huge potential for faux pas. This really took place in two distinct waves. Nowadays, many households in the UK are likely to have some wine glasses in the kitchen cupboards, but this wasn't the case back in the 1960s. Then in the 1970s the major petrol retailers started giving away wine glasses in gift-with-purchase promotions. Posh-looking ones too. Obviously, they weren't actually posh, but they looked like crystal, and people loved them. My parents collected them, and clearing their house out a few years ago, I found some, and was struck by how incredibly small they were. There was also the phenomenon of Green Shield Stamps, which probably won't mean anything to anyone younger than about 55. Basically, this was an analogue loyalty card, a bit like the early incarnation of the Nectar card here in the UK. A wide range of retailers gave shoppers Green Shield Stamps. Consumers collected the stamps and stuck them into books and were then able to swap completed books for a range of gifts. One of the most popular gifts was sets of wine glasses.

Now a new demographic had wine glasses in their homes, they needed some wine to pour into them. Changes in the law in England and Wales meant that it was now easier to buy wine to drink at home, and the alcohol industry was quick to respond by introducing a range of 'entry level' brands, such as Blue Nun and Mateus Rosé, with its distinctively shaped bottle which lent itself well to becoming a table lamp once empty. The key thing with these new wines was that consumers simply bought into the brand, and there was no need for them to know anything about grape varieties, country or region of origin, or vintages. With this barrier removed, consumers responded with enthusiasm and sales of wine increased almost ten-fold in 30 years (see Table 4.1).

Table 4.1: Average wine consumption per head in UK

Year	Average pint of wine per head per year	% change versus 1960
1960	3.6	–
1970	7.0	+194
1980	17.9	+497
1990	32.1	+891

Source: 'Continental Connotations': European Wine Consumption in 1970's Britain, Cambridge University Press, November 2020

The second wave of wine-democratization happened earlier this century. By this time, further changes in the law had made alcohol considerably more accessible, allowing it to be sold in corner shops and petrol stations, and at virtually any time of day or night. The marketing people realized that the generation of working-class young women who had cut their drinking teeth on alco-pops needed something to graduate to. When they went 'out out', they would generally drink spirits, but what about the quiet nights in with the girls? Gone were the days when they would natter over tea and biscuits. Enter a raft of highly accessible wine brands targeted very overtly at these young women who were apprehensive about choosing a wine they liked. There was no need to bother about grape varieties or where the wine came from – just go for the appealing label and a feminine name, 'Blossom Hill', 'Sun Goddess', 'Barefoot' or (very overt in its targeting, this one), 'Black Girl Magic'. These brands were very successful, both in terms of revenue, and in terms of bringing new drinkers into the market. But it seems the bubble may have burst – wine drinking is generally in decline, with older drinkers (65+) accounting for an increasing proportion of regular wine drinkers (up from 22% to 27% over the five years of 2015–2020) according to analysis by International Wine and Spirits Research, the leading source of data and analysis on the alcoholic beverage market. This tallies with the data we see from the NHS, that 42% of young women (and 34% of young men) aged 16–24 do not drink alcohol or have not done so in the last 12 months.

The tide really does seem to be changing, which is good news.

Low- and no-alcohol brands are growing

The growth of low- or no-alcohol brands has been a very welcome development. This started with beers, and in recent years we have seen the range and quality increase hugely. So too has the distribution and with it the 'acceptability' of these brands. It is a long time since I went to a pub and was unable to get an alcohol-free beer, and it is now normal to have a choice, which is fantastic. I also love that there is now some really good advertising for zero beers. Heineken 0.0's TV ad features a young driver being pulled over by the police. He assumes that they want to remonstrate with him for apparently drinking beer whilst driving, and is very smug, because the police have made a mistake because he is actually drinking a zero-alcohol beer. The engaging twist at the end is that the police officer is actually pointing out a parking infringement.

The first alcohol-free spirit I was aware of was Seedlip, and I was so excited to read about it. I immediately bought all three variants, and just love them. The packaging and labelling are as sophisticated as the taste, and I have absolutely no problem with paying the same for these as I would for an alcoholic spirit. I am delighted that entrepreneurs who are developing a delicious alcohol-free product are making good profits. Seedlip sells for similar prices to regular alcoholic spirits, but of course there is no excise duty to pay, so the margins are excellent. Good on them, I say. I know that these brands are expensive, but because they are not alcoholic and therefore not addictive, the bottles tend to last a lot longer. And there are no hidden costs (taxis, drunken take-aways, etc.) like there are with alcoholic spirits. There are now many alternatives to Seedlip on the market, with new ones being launched all the time and it really is so welcome to be able to drink a non-alcoholic drink that's not full of sugar and isn't aimed at children.

In my view, alcohol-free wines are still not there. There are some very palatable alternatives to Champagne or Prosecco – we had a delicious brand called Noughty for the non-drinkers at my daughter's wedding recently, and Nozeco is also really good. But I have yet to find a non-alcoholic still wine that I really like. There is a difference between non-alcoholic wine (which may never have been very alcoholic in the first place) and de-alcoholized wine, which is made by fermenting wine in the normal way, and then removing the alcohol through various methods such as vacuum distillation, centrifugation, or filtration. I am told by the aficionados that de- alcoholized wine tastes more like the 'real' thing but I have rarely come across any. I suspect that as the demand increases, we will see more of it. But for the moment, I am delighted to see so many palatable non-alcoholic options on the market.

It is really encouraging to see that consumption of low and no-alcohol products is increasing. In January 2024, the UK's most upmarket grocer, Waitrose, reported in their customer magazine that their sales of 'low and no' drinks had risen by 29% in 2023. According to YouGov research in 2022, around two-thirds of UK adults have tried a low- or no-alcohol product, and 26% of people say that their weekly alcohol consumption has decreased since they first tried low- or no-alcohol alternatives. The majority of those who drink these low-/no-alcohol products do also drink alcohol (78% versus 22% who never drink alcohol), but amongst younger age groups, there is a higher proportion who never drink alcohol (30% amongst 18–24 year olds). It seems that the young are indeed more 'generation sober' than is the case for previous generations, and that is to be welcomed![17]

Increase frequency (and/or volume)

The second way that the alcohol manufacturers increase their sales is to get those of us who drink alcohol to drink more of it. Here in the UK, alcohol manufacturers and retailers are regulated by the Portman Group which promotes responsible drinking and ensures high standards in the packaging, marketing, and advertising of alcohol. It is worth noting that the Portman Group regulations are advisory and not legally binding. However, it does actually work well as a self-policing industry body, and where there is a breach of the code of conduct, it is usually corrected quickly and efficiently.

The Portman Group Code of Practice includes the following stipulations that refer (directly or indirectly) to the amount of alcohol someone might consume, and seek to prevent people from being encouraged to drink more than they otherwise would/more than is sensible, in the hope of an (unlikely) outcome. Alcohol manufacturers are required to make sure that they do not:

- suggest any association with sexual activity or sexual success;
- suggest that consumption of the drink can lead to social success or popularity;
- encourage illegal, irresponsible, or immoderate consumption such as drink-driving, binge-drinking, or drunkenness;
- urge the consumer to drink rapidly or 'down' a product in one;
- suggest that the product has therapeutic qualities, can enhance mental or physical capabilities, or change mood or behaviour.

---

[17] YouGov research for the Portman Group.

Flagrant breaches of the Code of Practice are actually quite rare and are more commonly associated with packaging than marketing or advertising. The industry would claim that the guidelines show that it is definitely not encouraging excessive drinking. However, there are still plenty of ways in which people are encouraged to drink more/more often. One of the most egregious of these, to my mind, is the concept of the 'Happy Hour', when drinks are discounted for one hour, typically early in the evening. The idea is that drinkers should drink more than they otherwise would during that one hour, in order to make the most of the discounted prices. By the end of the hour, when the prices go back up again, they are likely to already be drunk, or well on their way to being drunk. Their judgement will be impaired and they are likely to go on to drink more than is sensible. In my opinion 'Happy Hours' should be banned and they most certainly shouldn't be called 'Happy' hours when they are directly contributing to alcohol abuse or dependence and all of the unhappiness that brings with it.

Happy Hours are just one way that landlords and bar owners can encourage people to drink more. Another is to offer free nibbles at certain times of day when the pub or bar might otherwise be quiet. There's many a pub that offers free snacks in the early evening, or on Sunday lunchtimes, and when they are gone, they are gone, thus encouraging people to come in earlier. The landlords know perfectly well that for a proportion of their customers, the earlier they can get them in, the more they'll drink.

But it isn't just the on-trade (pubs, clubs, and bars) that are to blame for encouraging people to drink more/more often. Retailers bear just as much responsibility, using cut-price alcohol as a loss-leader to encourage people into their stores. I have recently been coaching a lovely nurse whose alcohol dependence worsened significantly during the pandemic. Her tipple of choice is Prosecco, and when she told me how much she was drinking, I was curious about how she was affording this on a nurse's salary. She told me that she shops around. Every week, one of the supermarkets will have a really good deal on Prosecco, offering six bottles for well under £30. Whichever supermarket has the best deal, that's where she does that week's shopping. And as she pointed out, if you've got a problem with drinking, it is very hard to have six bottles in the house and not touch them. These deals are really not helpful, and I would love to see minimum pricing bought in throughout the UK and not just in Scotland. I'd also like to see a ban on any deals which encourage stockpiling. Selling alcohol at below cost price is exploitative and immoral, and in my view it should be illegal.

But sometimes no one is to 'blame' for things that lead to increased drinking. Trends emerge. Things just become fashionable for a while. A few years ago, 'Jäeger Bombs' were a big thing. They are the combination of Jäegermeister with an energy drink. They were never really my thing, as I had stopped drinking by the time they really caught on. I'm told that although their popularity has waned, they are still popular on university campuses. Back in my twenties, no meal in an Italian restaurant was complete without a flaming Sambuca, or maybe a limoncello. And the coffee-flavoured liqueur, Kahlua, was popular too; it's interesting how many of these trends revolve around alcoholizing coffee. And of course, these strong spirits are typically drunk at the end of an evening where people have arguably already had enough to drink.

Some of these trends, like the current popularity of Aperol Spritz, are not overly concerning as they are effectively the substitution of one drink for another. The trends that concern me are the ones which lead to increased drinking, where small volumes of strong alcohol are consumed on top of 'regular' drinks. These are often an addition to a non-alcoholic food or drink. For example, in the last few years, Espresso Martinis seem to be having a moment, where Martini is added to coffee. And it has become common for Affogato to have a shot of a liqueur added to the traditional mix of coffee and ice cream. Amongst my children and their friends, Craig Davids are a thing – a shot of Tequila followed by a tiny shot of harmless pineapple juice. Apparently, the name comes from the fact that the combination is 'surprisingly smooth', like the man himself, whilst some maintain that it is his favourite drink – I haven't been able to check this! What is clear is that by the time this book is out, there will be another alcoholic drink of choice available.

One final trend to note is how the internet has helped challenges to go viral. Some of these challenges have been altruistic, such as the Ice Bucket Challenge which raised huge amounts of money for the ALS Association (ALS is also known as motor neurone disease). But others have been less desirable, encouraging excessive and dangerous drinking. One such was the 2014 'neknomination' craze, challenging people to film themselves drinking a pint of an alcoholic drink in one gulp, and upload the footage on social media. It is believed to have led to at least five deaths.

The myth that alcohol relieves stress

Western society has a lot of beliefs about alcohol which do not stand up to scrutiny. One such is that it is great for unwinding and relieving stress. Well, to be fair, this is partially true – it does relieve stress and make us feel good for 20–30 minutes, thanks to a neurotransmitter called dopamine. But after that short period, it actually makes stress and anxiety worse. Alcohol is a chemical and its presence in the bloodstream leads to stimulation of the adrenal gland, and the release of cortisol and adrenaline. These are the hormones related to the fight or flight response. Which is fine if we find ourselves needing to use speed or strength to deal with a physical threat. But these situations are few and far between in modern life. Most of the time the threats we face are psychological, and the excess of cortisol and adrenalin in the bloodstream is not helpful.

The product we drink to relieve stress is actually making it worse. That is an unavoidable biological fact. The degree to which this is true will vary according to each individual's metabolism, but drinking alcohol will always make stress worse and not better.

We have a long way to go before we turn around the widely held belief that alcohol is an effective way to relieve stress, and as an employer, you have an important role to play in accelerating this change of perception. I believe that education about the effects of alcohol should be an integral part of every stress management programme.

The pressure to drink alcohol to fit in

As a society, we have really messed things up when it comes to alcohol. It is known to be a highly addictive substance, yet our society positively encourages its consumption, and it is the only drug where we have to explain why we are not taking it. Can you imagine going to a party where someone offers you some heroin, and when you refuse, they tell you not to be so boring and anti-social? It's unthinkable, but that is what happens with alcohol. And the cultural clues telling us to drink are everywhere. It's very difficult to buy an 18th birthday card that doesn't make reference to being legally able to drink. The internet is full of memes about the 'mummy wine culture', and our language just normalizes alcohol's role in our lives. We talk about 'wetting the baby's head', we 'raise a glass' whenever there's good news, and 'drown our sorrows' when there's bad news. We bond with colleagues over a beer after work, and a huge amount of client entertaining revolves around alcohol.

So, we have created a situation in which we encourage people to drink an addictive substance and make them feel excluded if they choose not to. And then comes the really contrary part.

The shame and stigma of alcohol addiction

When people become addicted to the addictive substance that society has been encouraging them to drink, they are stigmatized and shamed. They are made to believe it is their fault, that there is something flawed in them, that they are somehow different from so-called 'normal drinkers'. They are terrified that people will find out – hence the emphasis on anonymity in Alcoholics Anonymous. They fear being ostracized socially. In the work context, they fear that their careers will stall if they 'admit' to a problem with alcohol, or (depending on their contract) that they may actually be fired. This is something that people mostly try and sort out on their own, weighed down by shame.

And there is a widespread belief (perpetuated, I'm afraid, by AA), that once an alcoholic, always an alcoholic. This means that even if someone successfully becomes alcohol-free, they are forever tainted by their past addiction. I should know. By 'outing' myself as a former problem drinker, I come up against this all the time. I observe people literally and metaphorically take a step back, as though addiction were contagious. Or even worse, they step forward, eager to get the gory details of my rock bottom, so as to have some juicy gossip to pass on.

At one level, it is quite reasonable to be wary of having people in the workplace who are known to have a problem with alcohol. Alcohol impairs our co-ordination and our judgement, and so if someone is drunk at work, they represent a danger to others and to the organization. And of course, a heavy session can mean that someone's performance is still impaired the next day. And even if they are not over the limit the next day, a bad hangover will certainly make an individual much less productive. And generally, the drop in productivity will have a ripple effect. The hungover boss will not be so diligent checking the figures, so mistakes are more likely. They may be short-tempered and may damage team morale. They will probably be desperate to get home at the end of the day instead of maybe staying to finish off what they were doing.

Employers, like society at large, are generally wary of 'alcoholics' – if they are still drinking, the question will be 'Why can't they just pull themselves together?' And if someone has completely stopped drinking, the common term is that they are 'in recovery' rather than 'recovered'. This implies a lack of permanence, raising fears they could pick up a drink again at any time. These are flawed, defective people who are different from the rest of the population. Given that AA is by far the best-known resource, it is unsurprising that their view is so widespread. But it is not helpful.

People who lose control over alcohol feel immense shame. It is the most common emotion that we discuss in coaching – that and the self-loathing that accompanies it. And what do we do when we feel shame? We keep it secret. We don't want other people to know about the thing we're ashamed of. If they find out, they'll reject us (or fire us).

The fact that there is so much stigma, shame, and secrecy around problem drinking makes it very difficult for employers to help people who are struggling. Suggesting that an employee might have a problem with alcohol is a big deal.

The widely held (yet erroneous) belief that an 'alcoholic' is always recovering and never recovered, and therefore always at risk of relapse makes it difficult for a manager to ever fully trust that individual. Keeping them on is risky and could backfire. And so, this awful cloud of shame is perpetuated.

Chapter summary

- The alcohol industry and its advertising and marketing agencies have shaped the culture around drinking, bringing new people into the market, and encouraging us all to drink more/more frequently.

- Whilst there is encouraging news in the increasing sales of low- and no-alcohol drinks, there are nonetheless many people who turn to alcohol as a form of self-medication, mistakenly believing that it will help them to deal with stress, and who go on to develop AUD. The reality is that alcohol can only ever 'work' as a stress reliever for 20–30 minutes. After that period, the chemical reactions in the body mean that it leads to sadness, depression, stress, and anxiety.

- Although society encourages us to drink alcohol, it tends to shun anyone who develops an addiction to this addictive substance, leading to tragic levels of shame and stigma, which hold people back from asking for the help they need.

5

Why business leaders hold back from changing their organization's alcohol culture... seen as the fight we don't need to have

For many organizations, raising the topic of their culture and practices around alcohol is like kicking the hornets' nest; it feels like picking a fight that doesn't need to happen. Except that it *does* actually need to happen, for all of the reasons I've already discussed. So why the reticence?

Hypocrisy

I spoke to a few people who had needed to have a conversation with an employee about their problematic drinking, and here are a few of the things that were said in reply:

> There's nothing wrong with having a drink now and again.

> It's not illegal to have a drink, you know.

> That's rich coming from you... the state of you at the Christmas party last year!

> Well, if you don't want us to drink alcohol, you shouldn't have a bar in the building.

But you are always encouraging us to come to the pub and you buy the drinks. Are you saying it's ok for you to drink but not me?

There are two themes there – one is the universality of drinking alcohol. The other is hypocrisy. Both are holding organizations back from tackling the issue. An employer trying to raise awareness of the addictive nature of alcohol is countercultural. No one is doing it. And one of the reasons they're not doing it is because they feel hypocritical if they do. Some three-quarters (according to NHS data) of adults in this country drink, so it follows that the vast majority of bosses drink. And they have probably got drunk a few times. A fair few of them are likely to be problem drinkers themselves. This really is a case of 'people in glass houses shouldn't throw stones'.

By definition, hypocrisy involves someone being judged for doing something wrong, when the judger is also guilty of the same misdemeanour. Therein lies the problem. In Western society, there is nothing wrong with drinking alcohol – indeed it is positively encouraged. But we have made it wrong to drink too much of it, and to be unable to control our intake, without understanding the inevitability of some people becoming addicted to an addictive substance.

Reluctance to ask for help

The problem, I believe, is that alcohol is treated as a disciplinary issue, when it should be a wellbeing issue. The mental health movement is doing a great job in de-stigmatizing afflictions such as stress, anxiety, and depression. We no longer think that someone should just 'pull themselves together' because we understand that the causes of mental health crises are complex, and that sufferers need help and not judgement. Exactly the same thing applies when it comes to alcohol dependency. The causes are complex and telling someone who is addicted to 'just stop drinking' is ridiculous and massively unhelpful, and likely to elicit the response 'Don't you think I would stop if I could?'

People who have become dependent on alcohol need help, but they are afraid to ask their employer for this help. They may be afraid of their career stalling or even ending. They may be afraid of being vilified and shamed, of being made to feel inadequate and of being blamed. But where is the shame in becoming addicted to an addictive substance which is heavily promoted and completely ingrained in our culture? How different could things be if people felt comfortable asking for help, knowing that they would be treated compassionately and would not be jeopardizing their career development? Only a few years ago, women in their 50s suffered in silence at work as they battled the symptoms of the menopause. Hot flushes and mood swings were taboo subjects. But thanks to recent high-profile campaigns led by courageous women like Davina McCall, there is far greater awareness and understanding. We need to achieve the same thing for alcohol. And we need some courageous people to lead the way.

Debunking the myth that alcohol = fun

The alcohol industry has worked very hard to build an association between booze and fun. Have you ever seen anyone unattractive, sad, or lonely in an alcohol ad? Have you ever come across a bar promoting their 'unhappy hour'? Have you ever told a friend doing 'Dry January' not to be so boring?

Society and our culture tell us that alcohol makes us socially attractive and fun. But the reality is that excessive drinking leads to physical, mental, and emotional harm and it causes great unhappiness. The real bore is not the person who goes home sober at the end of the night, but the one who repeats themselves over and over again, increasingly incoherently, or who becomes maudlin or aggressive as the night wears on. Alcohol disinhibits us, and we do things which we wouldn't do when sober. And that can actually be very dangerous – the Hangover films are very funny but real life isn't like Hollywood. Bad things can happen when people are very drunk. Here are some things that have happened to people I know in my personal life (not through coaching):

- Drink-driving convictions.
- Had to go to hospital after an alcohol-related accident.
- Killed themselves by crashing a car whilst significantly over the limit (three people I know).
- Divorced by a partner who could no longer tolerate their alcohol-fuelled behaviour.
- Lost their job due to drinking.
- Severe financial problems.
- Suspected rape (horrific for both victim and perpetrator).
- Waking up next to someone, unsure of who the person is or what happened the previous evening.
- Unplanned pregnancies.
- Sexually transmitted diseases after sleeping with people they barely knew.
- Blackouts.
- Accidental death.
- Premature death due to alcoholic seizures.

None of this sounds like fun to me. And none of those things would have happened without alcohol in the mix. None of them.

But still, we perpetuate this myth that drinking alcohol makes us more fun to be with. And we castigate anyone who suggests otherwise, casting them as the 'Fun Police'.

Free will

We have rights. Of course we do. In most countries, we are free to express ourselves and to do what we like as long as it does not hurt other people. And that includes getting horribly drunk. As long as we don't injure someone, or commit a criminal act, we can pretty much drink what we want. And it is certainly not your place as an employer to curtail this. However, in exercising this right, there are a few things everyone needs to be aware of:

- If we hurt someone else when drunk, our drunkenness is not an excuse, and we may still be guilty of assault, or worse. Alcohol does not release us from being responsible for our own actions. Ask anyone who has been convicted of a serious crime when drunk. Ask any parent whose child has been killed or maimed by a drunk driver. Being drunk is not, and can never be, an excuse for criminal behaviour.

- Even if we do no physical harm to others when drunk, we may well cause significant offence to others and do lasting damage to our relationships. This can be through what we say or how we behave. It would be interesting to know how much infidelity is fuelled by alcohol – I expect it's a very high proportion.

- Very often, the person we are hurting the most through our drinking is ourselves. Physically, mentally, and emotionally, alcohol does us no favours at all.

- Alcohol impairs our performance and may well impact the quality of our work, which is likely to impact our career progression if we don't do something about the drinking.

Confidentiality

In the context of alcohol, there is another important right that we have, and that is a right to confidentiality as and when our drinking becomes a problem. This is enshrined in law. There comes a point (admittedly, quite a blurry and indistinct point, but a point nonetheless) when a person's dependence on alcohol becomes a medical issue. And of course, the medical profession is legally bound to keep all patient information confidential and can only discuss a patient's condition with the express permission of that patient. Even if someone's drinking is not yet known by their doctor, the fact that they feel they may have a problem should remain confidential, until such time as they choose to share it. And let's be realistic, in the current climate, they are pretty unlikely to share it. There is, currently, huge shame and stigma attached to developing a problem with alcohol. I wish with all my heart that this wasn't true, but it is. It's why Alcoholics Anonymous is just that… anonymous.

Please don't misunderstand me. I am 100% not arguing that the right to confidentiality should be waived or that confidentiality rules should be broken. Absolutely not.

What I am saying, however, is that the shame and guilt around alcohol dependency is exacerbated and, to a degree, perpetuated, by confidentiality. There are very few examples of people who have, for want of a better phrase, 'come out' as having overcome issues with alcohol before going on to build successful careers. Yet the rooms of AA and the client lists of private coaches and rehab clinics are full of senior leaders who have successfully put their alcohol addiction problems behind them. But those people keep quiet about it. Hardly anyone knows and those who do are sworn to secrecy. Which means that no one is able to draw inspiration from their story. The people who work for them have no idea that the boss used to have a problem. They don't feel confident sharing their truth for fear of judgement and stalling, or possibly even ending their career.

Inevitably, most of the reformed drinkers we hear about are famous, and we hear about their stories through the media. They tend to come from the world of entertainment, where their 'brand' will not be tarnished by revealing past problems with alcohol. Indeed, drugs and alcohol have long been seen as part and parcel of the creative or rock 'n' roll lifestyle, part of the 'bad boy' or 'wild child' image. And there is respect and admiration for former addicts for addressing their addictions. Quite right too, because overcoming a dependence on an addictive substance is difficult. But it seems to me that it is much harder for people in 'conventional' jobs to identify themselves as having, or having had, a problem with alcohol, than it is for famous people from the world of entertainment. This is because in more conventional jobs, having had a problem with alcohol is seen as something of a risk factor. The 'once an alcoholic, always an alcoholic' school of thought is erroneous, but widely held, and so employers are concerned that the alcoholic may relapse at some stage, causing problems for said employer. A singer or an actor who relapses is really only harming themselves and their immediate entourage.

But if an executive in an insurance company, for example, were to have a serious relapse, then they could cause serious commercial and reputational damage to the company.

Secrecy begets secrecy

The big issue we are dealing with here is the stigma and shame around alcohol dependence amongst workers. It means that even decades after their last drink, people who have overcome AUD stay silent, terrified that their 'guilty secret' will come out and jeopardize their career. This silence and the lack of visible role models means that anyone in the throes of developing AUD will stay silent too. They will struggle and try to sort it out themselves, because asking for help would mean telling someone what is going on, and once someone else knows, there is the risk that their employer will find out.

Leaders need to lead on this

How different could things be if we set aside the stigma and judgement around AUD in the same way that there is now open dialogue about mental health issues, and issues around the menopause? Imagine if there was widespread compassion for anyone with AUD, and an understanding that this had happened simply because they are a human being, and not because they are a *defective* human being. Imagine if everyone who had overcome AUD felt safe to talk openly about what had happened to them, and how they had been able to turn things around. Imagine how uplifting it would be for an employee concerned about their drinking to be able to go and chat with someone in the organization who was an ambassador for getting help early. For that employee, how reassuring would it be to know that they would be met with compassion and practical suggestions for a funded pathway out of AUD, instead of judgement and recrimination. For that to happen, we need to build *trust*. And trust is a leadership issue. We need senior people in every organization to lead the way. If every Board pledged to do away with the stigma, it could happen very quickly. If every Board Member who has had any level of AUD were to go public about it and offer a compassionate listening ear to others in their organization, more junior members of staff would start to feel safe asking for help. If a Board Member can retain their prominent position, despite having a history of AUD, then perhaps the organization really *is* changing. Perhaps it *is* safe to ask for help. Perhaps doing so will be career-enhancing (allowing someone to get back to their best), rather than career-limiting or career-ending.

This book includes a Charter for Change (see Chapter 11), which is intended as a blueprint for how your organization can go about changing the culture around alcohol. One suggestion is to use key dates in the calendar, such as Mental Health Awareness Week or Alcohol Awareness Week, to get senior people within the organization to talk publicly about their own challenges with alcohol, and to encourage a more open and compassionate attitude across the organization. For this to be effective, employees will need to genuinely trust the leadership team to deliver on a promise to help and not vilify those in need of help. It may take time to establish that trust. But if senior leaders can be consistent, it will be established, and the organization will be all the better for it. A key part of achieving this will be for there to be a much better understanding of addiction, and that is what I will cover in the next chapter.

Chapter summary

- Business leaders are loathe to raise the subject of changing the alcohol culture in their organizations because most of them enjoy a drink every now and again and they fear being seen as hypocrites.

- Changing the alcohol culture is not currently on many (or any) board agendas unless it is in the context of disciplinary issues. It needs to be treated as a wellbeing issue rather than a disciplinary one.

- Forward-thinking businesses which care about their employees' wellbeing will include alcohol-education as a key plank in their wellbeing programmes and will help to dispel the myth that alcohol is an essential ingredient for having fun – it is not.

- Business leaders need to demonstrate that it is safe for people to come forward and ask for help, by leading from the front, sharing their own stories and experiences in order to create an environment of safety and trust.

- Confidentiality must be respected, but individuals will be more likely to be open about their problems with alcohol once they know that discussing this will not jeopardize their career in any way.

PART 2

Understanding why people become dependent on alcohol

6

Why do some people develop AUD but not others?

Close your eyes for a minute, and visualize an alcoholic. How are they dressed? What is their hair like? How do they smell? Where are they? What do they do all day? Where do they live?

I suspect that you visualized a down-and-out, very scruffily dressed, unkempt hair, living on the streets having lost their job, their family, and their home. They may have been sitting on the park bench swigging straight from the can or bottle. Or you may have visualized them begging for money – they'll say it is for food for them or their dog, but you are pretty sure that any money you give them will be spent on booze.

That description certainly fits someone in the more advanced stage of AUD. But it is probably a million miles away from how you see yourself or any of your colleagues. The thing is that addiction to alcohol is progressive. It creeps up on us. Not on everyone, it is true, but on a fair few. There are theories about a tendency to addiction being genetic, but scientists have yet to discover any addiction gene (despite years of trying).

Not everyone who drinks will develop AUD. And not everyone who develops AUD will land up on the streets. But too many do. And we need to realize that the earlier someone gets help, the less pronounced their AUD will become and the quicker they will be able to put it behind them and go on to live a happy and productive life.

When people become addicted to the addictive substance that society has been encouraging them to drink, they are stigmatized and shamed. They are made to believe it is their fault, that there is something flawed in them, that they are somehow different from so-called 'normal drinkers'. This is indeed a core tenet of Alcoholics Anonymous (AA), and is one of the things that concerns me. This belief that the 'alcoholic' is flawed has caused so much misery and self-loathing. It is also why there is a substantial proportion of people for whom AA simply doesn't work.

AA talks of problem drinkers ('alcoholics', in their language) being different from 'normal drinkers', and it is certainly true that there is a difference between someone suffering from full-blown AUD and the casual, take-it-or-leave-it social drinker.

There are two key points to understand:

1. This is an *everyone* problem, in that it can happen to anyone, anyone at all. And it is not their fault. That is really important, so I'll say it again. *It is not their fault.* The person who develops AUD is not defective or flawed. They're human.
2. AUD is not permanent, and recovery IS possible – full recovery where people are able to live happy and fulfilled lives without even thinking about alcohol.

Why should you believe this explanation of alcohol addiction, rather than the 'fatal flaw' theory?

- It is backed by science.
- It offers genuine and sustainable hope to sufferers.
- It empowers people to take control and turn things around.
- It is supported by evidence (see Chapter 12 for details).

Trauma and genetics

I'd like to dig a bit deeper into this idea that this can happen to anyone, and into the impact of trauma and genetics.

Earlier, I discussed how trauma can be the thing that tips a 'social' drinker into problematic drinking. But what do we mean by 'trauma'? It's a bit of a loaded word, and I actually don't use it in coaching any more. One person's trauma is another person's 'tough times' – both can trigger a slide into AUD. And of course, there is no reason why you, as an employer, would know anything about the past traumas in your employees' lives.

We know that people who suffer from various forms of trauma or mental health crises are more likely to develop AUD or other addictions. And to an extent, this can be generational.

Genetic tendency[18] – It is fair to say that there is significant academic debate about the degree to which alcohol dependence is genetic. Let me summarize the science. The idea that there is a single gene which determines whether or not someone will develop AUD is false. It's not like Huntington's disease, where, if one particular gene is defective, you'll get the disease. But that is not to say that there is no genetic component at all.

Recent genome studies support a polygenic model for alcohol dependence. This means that there are a number of different genes that contribute to alcohol dependence, each having a relatively minor effect. The more of these genes that an individual has, the greater the genetic risk factor for them developing AUD. However, the research also showed that what happens in someone's upbringing (i.e., nurture) is a better predictor for alcohol dependence than the sum of genetic risk variants (i.e., nature). The truth is that we still don't understand the full story when it comes to genetics and alcohol dependence, and it is clear that environmental factors are also important. We can see the combination of genetics and environmental factors at play if we look at twin studies.[19] These are studies into twins, both fraternal (who typically share around 50% of their DNA) and identical twins, who have exactly the same genetic code, exactly the same DNA.

[18] https://jmolecularpsychiatry.biomedcentral.com/articles/10.1186/2049-9256-1-11#:~:text=Genetic%20as%20well%20as%20environmental,DNA%20methylation%20at%20CpG%20sites

[19] www.cambridge.org/core/journals/twin-research-and-human-genetics/article/minnesota-twin-family-study/D30DD0AD62A9D6869428E57A7C7F6025

The most famous twin study is the Minnesota Twin Family Study, which began in the 1970s and continued for several decades. This showed that even identical twins who shared the same genetic makeup could have different outcomes with respect to alcohol dependence if they were exposed to different environmental influences. The study differentiated between shared environmental factors (such as family upbringing) and non-shared environmental factors (experiences unique to each twin, such as different peer groups and life experiences), and the results showed that non-shared environmental factors had a more significant impact on alcohol dependence than shared environmental factors. The most significant of these non-shared environmental factors were:

- **Peer group influence:** Differences in the choice of friends and peer groups can have a big impact on an individual's use or abuse of alcohol. Twins may have different sets of friends and different social circles, which will lead to varying levels of exposure to alcohol-related behaviours.

- **Life events:** Unique life events, such as traumatic experiences, job changes, or issues in relationships can influence an individual's alcohol consumption. For example, if one identical twin is happily married and the other is in an abusive relationship with a heavy drinker, the latter is the more likely of the two to develop AUD.

- **Access to alcohol:** Twins are mostly brought up together, but as they become independent, their living arrangements and circumstances will vary. The study shows that easy access to alcohol increases the risk of AUD.

- **Parenting style:** The number of identical twins who are brought up separately from each other is small, but there may be a difference in parenting style even when identical twins are brought up together, and the data support the significance of this when it comes to AUD.

- **Education and occupation:** Twins may pursue different educational paths or career choices, leading to variations in their exposure to alcohol-related settings and stressors.

And these, in turn, can influence alcohol consumption and the risk of AUD.

- **Cultural and religious influences:** Differences in cultural backgrounds and religious beliefs can affect an individual's attitudes towards alcohol and their likelihood of consuming it. Twins with differing cultural or religious affiliation (whether from childhood or later in life), may have distinct perspectives on alcohol use.

- **Psychological factors:** Unique psychological experiences and coping mechanisms can influence an individual's relationship with alcohol. Twins may have varying levels of stress, anxiety, or depression, which can affect their alcohol consumption differently.

In addition to genetics and environment, there is one other major influence on how likely a person is to develop AUD. And that is the complex area of epigenetics. This is the study of changes in gene expression that occur without changes to the underlying DNA sequence. These changes can be influenced by various factors such as environmental conditions, lifestyle, and even experiences. These can affect how genes are turned on or off, ultimately impacting our traits and characteristics. This means that external factors can influence the way that genes function and our biological inheritance goes beyond the genetic code.

The important thing to understand is that, even if there is, in you, a genetic tendency towards AUD, it does *not* mean that AUD is inevitable. With the right help at the right time, it is possible for anyone to change their relationship with alcohol and put their AUD firmly behind them. The idea that we might be genetically programmed to develop AUD is disempowering and very unhelpful.

The role of trauma in the development of AUD

It is worth noting that alcohol is often an intrinsic part of the trauma that leads an individual to drink. This is effectively learned behaviour – a parent who deals with unhappiness by drinking will inadvertently 'teach' their child to see alcohol as the way adults deal with unhappiness. That child is traumatized by the parent's drinking, and masks their feelings by drinking, and potentially develops AUD. Many would insist that this is due to genetics, but the science shows that nurture is as significant as nature, if not more so.

But by no means is all trauma alcohol related. And not everyone who suffers trauma goes on to develop AUD. The Muslim faith for example, prohibits drinking alcohol, and it is therefore uncommon to come across a Muslim who is suffering from AUD. Societal and cultural norms are a huge factor. It is culturally unacceptable for some faith groups to drink alcohol and this could result in a lack of cultural normalization of drinking to numb pain. These faith groups are likely to have developed alternative healthier ways of processing emotional pain, such as strong social cohesion and tight family groups.

AA versus *This Naked Mind* – the importance of choice

Next, I am going to look at the options for overcoming AUD, comparing the well-known Alcoholics Anonymous 12-step programme and the alternative *This Naked Mind* method. My aim is not to cast aspersions on AA, but to explain why it doesn't work for everyone, and to give some insight into the viable alternative of *This Naked Mind*'s methodology.

I spent a couple of years attending various AA meetings. Although I desperately wanted to put alcohol behind me, AA never felt right for me, for the following reasons:

- Despite being brought up a Catholic (or perhaps because I was brought up a Catholic), I have a bit of a problem with the whole God-thing in AA. Fair enough, they do talk about God or your Higher Power, but even so, it did make me feel that there is a white-haired, white-bearded individual somewhere 'up there' who is extremely annoyed with me.

- At the AA meetings I went to (and I tried a variety of meetings in three different towns over a period of around two years),

I was made to feel that I hadn't hit enough of a rock bottom. In the world of alcoholism, I was a lightweight, and it felt like I was being told to go away and come back when I was a more serious alcoholic with some juicier stories to tell – a night or two in a police cell, a serious alcohol-related injury, my husband leaving me or an employer firing me because of my drinking. No one actually said this in so many words, but it is how I felt when I listened to the stories of other people's death-defying rock bottoms. And knowing that alcohol addiction is progressive, I just wanted to get off that runaway train sooner rather than later.

- Because so many of the people at the meetings I went to had had pretty low rock bottoms, I felt I didn't fit in and didn't have a lot in common with them. It really does make the journey easier if you can find some like-minded people to travel with.

- When you speak at an AA meeting, you are encouraged to introduce yourself by saying 'Hello, my name is (Tabbin) and I'm an alcoholic'. If you want to, you can add how long it has been since your last drink, but that's not mandatory. I felt really uncomfortable labelling myself as an alcoholic, and I genuinely don't think this was down to me being in denial (as suggested by my would-be sponsor). If I was in denial, surely I wouldn't even be at an AA meeting, would I? I don't like labels at the best of times, but if I am going to label myself, I want a clear definition of whatever it is I am labelling myself as – and there isn't a universally accepted medical definition of alcoholism.

- But perhaps my biggest problem was the fact that AA considers alcoholics to be intrinsically flawed, and different from 'normal drinkers'. They talk of being 'powerless' in the face of this substance, and say that an alcoholic can never recover, but will always be 'in recovery'. So, AA would have me believe that I was intrinsically flawed and could do nothing about it apart from using willpower and the fellowship of AA to stay away from alcohol forever. I would probably need to attend meetings for the rest of my life and white-knuckle it to stay sober. No one was talking about why I liked to drink or how I could reduce or remove the desire to drink. It was just a case of 'don't do it' and that message just didn't do it for me. At the time when I was going to AA, I had never come across Annie Grace or the *This Naked Mind* methodology which would later prove to be so helpful to me. I hadn't come across Annie's argument that the problem is not the drinker, but the drink itself. Nor did I understand that it is possible to reframe our beliefs about alcohol so that we no longer want to drink. All of that joyous messaging was yet to come my way. All I knew at that stage was that AA felt negative and depressing, and they didn't seem to want me there anyway.

When I stop and think about AA now, all of these points still hold true, and there is one other thing to add. I have a problem with both of the words in the name Alcoholics Anonymous.

- **Alcoholic:** The problem I have with the word 'alcoholic' is that there is no agreed medical or scientific definition of what an alcoholic is, as you'll discover if you search 'Am I an alcoholic?' If you go to see a doctor for help, you'll be left having to determine for yourself whether you are an alcoholic. In fact, most doctors now refer to Alcohol Use Disorder rather than Alcoholism and I think that is helpful. A disorder implies a spectrum, whereas being an alcoholic sounds pretty binary (even though it clearly isn't). Alcoholism isn't defined by the quantity, frequency, or intensity of drinking. And nor is it defined by its consequences (health issues, blackouts, drink-driving convictions, broken relationships, or damaged careers). What it really comes down to is the amount of headspace it is taking up, how much of a pre-occupation it is. And that is subjective, hence the difficulty in coming up with a workable definition.

- **Anonymous:** The problem I have with the word 'anonymous' is not what it means, but that it should be applied in this context. Anonymity is reserved for things that are shameful or even criminal, things that we feel compelled to keep secret for fear of negative consequences. **I believe with every fibre in my body that becoming dependent on alcohol is nothing to be ashamed about.** The reality is that this stuff is addictive to human beings. Anyone who drinks enough of it will, progressively, find themselves addicted to it. We know that the people most likely to develop an addiction are those who are using alcohol to self-medicate or numb themselves from pain – usually emotional pain, but sometimes physical pain too. What is shameful about that? What is shameful about feeling painful emotions, or being in physical or mental pain? Nothing at all. What is shameful is that, as a society, we know that this stuff is addictive, and yet we encourage people to drink it, and then when the inevitable happens and some of them find themselves addicted to it, we shun them to the point that they feel the only way they can get help is anonymously. **The way out of the mess that we have created is not to perpetuate the need for anonymity, but for everyone who is suffering from AUD to feel safe speaking up and asking for the help they need without fear of negative consequences. We have a long way to go!**

AA believes that the difference between 'normal' drinkers and alcoholics is accounted for by an in-built and permanent defect in the heavy drinker. Another school of thought – the *This Naked Mind* methodology – challenges this, and the argument goes like this:

- Alcohol is a substance which is addictive to human beings.

- Any human being who drinks 'enough' of it, is liable to become addicted to it.

- The difference between not enough or enough to become addicted is not clear-cut or quantifiable, but a lot of research[20] indicates that a key determinant is whether

---

[20] *Adverse childhood experiences and personal alcohol abuse as an adult*, S.R. Dube et al.; *Impact of ACEs on adult alcohol consumption behaviours*, E. Loudermilk et al.

people are drinking to self-medicate or numb themselves from some form of emotional pain.

- The people most likely to drink enough alcohol to become addicted to it are those who drink to escape what is happening, or has happened to them, physically, mentally, or emotionally. Anyone who has suffered any of the following is at risk of using alcohol to self-medicate, which can quickly lead to dependence:
  - o abuse;
  - o extreme poverty;
  - o family breakdown;
  - o parent who drank heavily or abused substances;
  - o lack of connection particularly in early childhood;
  - o isolation;
  - o stress;
  - o anxiety;
  - o prolonged periods of danger or uncertainty;
  - o relationship breakdown;
  - o PTSD;
  - o low self-worth;
  - o grief and loss;
  - o abandonment;
  - o major illness;
  - o burnout (due to work or responsibilities caring for others);
  - o clinical depression.

The more of these risk factors that apply for someone, the greater their risk of developing an addiction to alcohol or another substance. As their employer, you are unlikely to know about your employees' past traumas. But you may well see the evidence. And you may, through an alcohol-centric culture, be contributing to their acceleration towards serious AUD.

The *This Naked Mind* (TNM) approach is based on the belief that there is nothing inherently wrong with the individual who develops AUD. Instead of focusing on the behaviour (i.e., the drinking), TNM coaches work with clients to help them to identify the beliefs they have about alcohol which are leading them to want to drink – things like 'it helps me to relax', 'I have more fun when I'm drinking', and 'I drink to be sociable'. Coaches use science to challenge the very foundation of these beliefs, so that clients are then able to reframe their thoughts and beliefs around alcohol, to the point where they no longer have any desire to drink. And once the desire to drink has been removed, there is no need to rely on willpower to remain alcohol-free.

Chapter summary

- Most people have pre-conceptions of alcoholism which are quite wide of the mark and are more typical of the final stages of AUD – alcoholics start off as normal social drinkers.

- There are differences of opinion amongst the 'experts' regarding the degree to which AUD is genetic or innate in someone's personality – AA believes that those who become addicted to alcohol are 'flawed' and different from 'normal' drinkers, whereas *This Naked Mind*'s belief is that anyone who drinks enough of this addictive substance will develop AUD.

- There are differences in the approach taken by AA and TNM, with some people flourishing through AA and others finding freedom with TNM – we are all different. The key thing is that those who get into difficulty with alcohol should have a choice about how they address their problems.

- There is definitely a genetic component to addiction, but it is an influencing factor, with nurture being arguably more important than nature.

- Trauma is also a very strong influence, and research shows that the more Adverse Childhood Experiences (ACEs) someone has had, the greater the risk that they will go on to develop AUD or other addictions.

7

Regardless of the differing beliefs about why dependence develops, the result is the same

In this chapter, I will shed some light on the nature of alcohol addiction, by explaining the chemical processes that go on in the brain when we drink alcohol. Whether you suffer from any degree of AUD yourself, or you have people in your workforce who do, it is helpful to understand exactly what is going on. Armed with this understanding, you will see why people can't just stop drinking, even though many of them will want to.

It's an 'acquired' taste

The strange irony about alcohol is that it actually tastes disgusting, or at least, pure alcohol does. We mix the pure alcohol with things to make it taste better, but even so, wine and beer can be pretty unappealing when we first drink them. In scientific experiments researching the effects of alcohol, it is necessary to add sugar to alcohol in order to make it palatable for rats. The alcohol manufacturers do pretty much the same thing for us humans, adding sugar and bright colours to 'alco-pops' to make the drinks appealing for those people who have yet to acquire the taste. But for humans and rats alike, it doesn't take long for us to 'acquire the taste'. And this is not because our tastebuds suddenly change, so that we start to like something that we previously didn't like. It is because of what is going on in our brain.

Our brain is quick to learn that drinking the unpleasant tasting liquid leads to the pleasant buzz we get from alcohol, those feelings of warmth, relaxation, and sociability. And another unpleasant aspect of drinking alcohol for the first time can be the feeling of burning as it goes down your throat, and this can be a very strong feeling if you are drinking spirits. But the brain very quickly associates the taste and the burning sensation with the effect, and hey presto, we start to like the taste and the burn. And it is not just the taste and the burning sensation that become associated with the pleasant buzz from alcohol. It can be the setting, the time of day, the event, the people we are with, even the glass we are drinking from. They all become associated with that 20–30 minute buzz, and they effectively act as triggers for us to drink. And once those associations are formed in the brain, we no longer need the added sweeteners to make the drink palatable, which is why we are able to move on from the 'entry level' alco-pops or sweet cider to more 'sophisticated' drinks which are often much more bitter to taste. And in the lab, the same thing happens with rats. Once they have experienced alcohol a few times, they associate it with pleasant feelings and will drink it without any added sugars, even though they rejected this before.

The chemical process that happens when we drink alcohol

The pleasant buzz that we get when we drink alcohol is caused by the release of the neurotransmitter **dopamine**. There is nothing wrong with dopamine, as long as it is produced naturally – it is a good thing, a pleasurable reward-chemical. But drinking alcohol, leads to the *artificial* stimulation of dopamine – and it doesn't end well. The alcohol enters the bloodstream, and our blood alcohol content (BAC) rises, along with the dopamine levels. But once the BAC starts to fall, after just 20–30 minutes, the body produces a counter-chemical called **dynorphin**. This is a downer, a depressant, with sedative effects and it sticks around for a lot longer – some 3–4 hours. And the kicker is that the dynorphin takes our mood lower than it was before we had the first drink – the exact amounts of euphoria and dysphoria will vary from person to person, and according to circumstances, but the pattern is always the same. Drinking alcohol will leave you feeling more depressed than you were before you had that first drink. And the more you drink, the lower your mood will be, which goes to explain why we can often end an evening of drinking feeling very miserable and maudlin. I have a clear memory (actually, not that clear, but a memory nonetheless) of being very drunk and in tears in a nightclub in London at the end of a work night out. At the time, I had no idea why I was so tearful. Now I understand that it was a chemical reaction to all the alcohol I had drunk – my system was effectively flooded with dynorphin.

Figure 7.1 is based on illustrative figures, just to show the process. When that dynorphin low hits after the first drink, we seek to correct it with a second/third/fourth drink – we are looking for the dopamine hit. But however much we drink, we cannot get back to the levels of happiness that we were enjoying before the first drink. Effectively, alcohol is lying to us – promising to make us feel better, but actually and inevitably, making us feel worse, and for many hours to come as the impact of the dynorphin is slow to wear off.

Figure 7.1: Alcohol is both a stimulant and a depressant

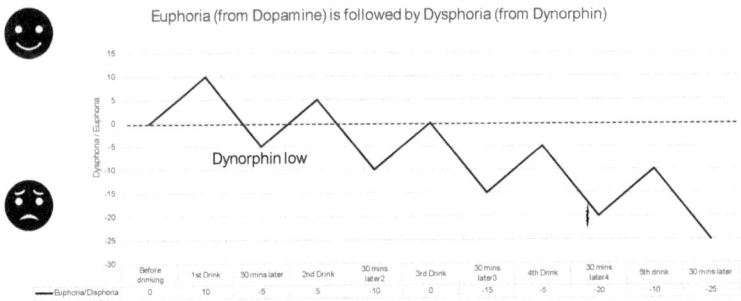

The chemical reaction set in train by drinking alcohol doesn't stop with the production of dynorphin. It also stimulates the adrenal gland, which produces the stress and anxiety hormones, **adrenaline** and **cortisol**. There is nothing inherently wrong with having these hormones in your system – cortisol is what gets us going in the morning, and a surge of adrenaline (the fight-or-flight hormone) can be very useful if you are facing a physical threat, giving you strength or speed that you wouldn't normally have. But if there is no physical threat, a few undesirable things can happen:

- Aggression and violence can result. Alcohol leads to mental impairment and loss of judgement and drunk people often perceive a threat where there is none, and they may pick a fight. This 'red mist' can lead to injuries and even fatalities, along with many criminal convictions. Indeed, the UK's Office for National Statistics reports that in 2019–2020, alcohol was linked to 42% of all violent crime.

- The body will be flooded with adrenalin and cortisol whilst the drinker is asleep or passed out, and the levels will peak sometime after their last drink. This explains why people will often wake at 3 or 4 in the morning after a night of drinking, feeling incredibly anxious, with racing heart and panicky feelings that make it hard to get back to sleep.

- The anxiety will last into the next day – there really is such a thing as 'hangxiety' or 'booze-anoia' and it is because of the excess cortisol and adrenalin which has been released because of the alcohol in the system.

- The dangers of long-term or repeated stress and anxiety include high blood pressure, risk of cardiovascular disease and stroke as well as digestive problems and type 2 diabetes.

It is also important to understand that it takes time for the body to process alcohol – roughly one hour for every unit or standard drink (and we need to use the UK definition of a unit here, i.e., 8 grams of pure alcohol or ½ pint of 4.5–5.0% ABV beer). The precise length of time depends on the individual and a variety of factors, but really the liver cannot do its job much faster than this. If there is too much alcohol in the bloodstream for the liver to process at any one time, it effectively keeps circulating until the liver can deal with it. This means that someone who drinks a bottle of wine in the evening (approximately nine units) will take around nine hours to process that alcohol. If they don't stop drinking until midnight, that alcohol won't be fully processed before 9am and they will still be intoxicated until then.

Cognitive dissonance

Cognitive dissonance is the technical term used to describe the contradictory feeling of wanting to do two things at the same time, that feeling of having two brains – one that knows you don't want to do something, and the other that pushes you to do it anyway. In effect there are two parts of our brain which are in opposition to each other, the subconscious and the pre-frontal cortex.

The subconscious is the instinctive part of our brain – strong on intuition but decidedly weak when it comes to intellect. The subconscious is irrational, in the sense that it is not capable of rational thought and can't process or analyse information. It is very basic and focused on survival and immediate pleasure/reward. It is not capable of analysing the consequences of any action.

The pre-frontal cortex is completely different. It is often described as the CEO of the brain, the intelligent, analytical part that differentiates humans as a species. It is able to complete complex processes, and to think through the consequences of any action.

When someone wakes up hungover and vowing not to drink that day, it is the pre-frontal cortex that is responsible for their analytical thinking – 'last night's alcohol consumption has me feeling ill today – I don't want to feel like this tomorrow morning so I will stay off the booze tonight'.

But as the day wears on, the individual is likely to start thinking about alcohol, and to find themselves with a beer or a glass of wine in their hand by the evening, even though they vowed not to. The decision to have that drink (or more likely those drinks) is prompted by the subconscious, which is focused purely on the very short-term pleasure to be derived from the alcohol.

The opposition between these two parts of the brain is very uncomfortable, and when the subconscious wins out, this leads to people beating themselves up for a lack of willpower. But in reality, the subconscious is massive and very powerful. In his book *Thinking, Fast and Slow*, Daniel Kahneman refers to the subconscious as System One (the primal, instinctive one) and System Two (which is rational and analytical). More visually, psychologist Jonathan Haidt compares the subconscious to a large elephant, and the pre-frontal cortex to a small man trying to ride that elephant. This is a great analogy, not just because it gives an indication of the relative size and power of each part of the brain, but also because it is clear that the man cannot force the elephant to do something, he has to persuade it. And so it is with the brain – it is much more effective to persuade the subconscious that it doesn't want to drink (by reframing beliefs around alcohol) than trying to force it not to drink (i.e., using willpower).

AUD is progressive, and that is down to the addictive nature of the substance. As you saw earlier in this chapter, the chemical reactions that occur in the body as result of drinking alcohol leave the drinker wanting more, in an effort to get back to the euphoria they felt after the first drink. The alcohol creates a demand for more. And as the drinker gradually drinks more and more over time, they find that their tolerance increases. It takes more alcohol for them to feel inebriated, and this is often seen as a badge of honour – you know the kind of thing – 'they can hold their drink', 'they've got hollow legs', 'they could drink anyone under the table'.

But this increased tolerance is not a good sign. It leads to the drinker needing more and more alcohol to get the desired effect, and that increased intake leads to increased health risks. The more that someone is drinking, the greater their risk of developing liver disease, cancer, and cardiovascular problems. And those are just the physical risks. They are also putting themselves at greater risk of suffering from stress, anxiety, and depression, which could then fuel more self-medicating with alcohol.

The pitcher plant analogy

In his book *The Easy Way to Control Alcohol*, Alan Carr uses the analogy of a pitcher plant to illustrate the progressive nature of AUD. The plant is shaped like a pitcher (or a jug). Like many plants, it has delicious-smelling nectar, and flies are attracted to it and start to feed themselves. But what they don't realize is that they are at the top of a very slight incline, which is covered in small hairs which all point in one direction allowing the insects to go down but not back up again. It's all very subtle, and the flies are so distracted by the delicious nectar that they don't even notice. But gradually the slope becomes steeper, and the flies become unnerved by the fact that they can't seem to get back out of the plant. They try desperately to get out, managing a few steps upwards before they fall back down even further. And they are even more unnerved when they realize that what smelled delicious when they were at the top is not quite as wonderful as they thought – the smell is actually the rotting and decomposing bodies of other flies that got trapped. They realize that, short of a miracle, there is only one way this is going to end for them – badly. It is a gruesome analogy, but one that most AUD sufferers agree is painfully accurate. Left to its own devices, this is a progressive condition. As an employer, you should be helping people to avoid it rather than encouraging it.

Chapter summary

- Pure alcohol tastes disgusting – we quite literally have to 'acquire' the taste for it, and this occurs when we start to associate the taste with the (very short-term) pleasurable effects of drinking.

- The first 20–30 minutes after a drink are indeed pleasurable – the buzz or high that we get from that dopamine hit is the reason we drink. But it doesn't last, it can't last. Once the alcohol gets into our bloodstream, it triggers a chemical process leading to the release of dynorphin (a depressant which sedates us), followed by the stimulation of the adrenal gland, triggering the release of cortisol and adrenalin, the stress and anxiety hormones.

- The phenomenon of wanting to drink whilst also wanting not to drink is known as cognitive dissonance – two parts of our brain (the subconscious and the pre-frontal cortex) are in direct opposition. The only way of permanently changing this is to change the subconscious thoughts and beliefs around alcohol, effectively re-wiring the brain, thus removing the subconscious desire to drink. The alternative strategy is to rely on willpower, but like an exhausted muscle, willpower tends to fail just when we need it the most.

- AUD is progressive as illustrated by the analogies of the runaway train and the pitcher plant. Employers who have turned a blind eye to the alcohol culture in their organization, or even encouraged their staff to drink, have a responsibility to help those people before their AUD becomes so advanced that it blights their life.

PART 3

What to do about it: assess, plan, implement, sustain

8

Looking in the mirror

It can be pretty difficult to know if your organization is bottling up trouble and being held back by alcohol. You may console yourself with the thought that the alcohol culture in the workplace is a lot healthier than it was a few years ago. There can be no doubt that this is true, but it doesn't mean that we are where we need to be.

Let's take a look at how much things have changed. When I first started out in advertising, in 1984, I worked for an agency with offices close to Paddington Station, and on the first floor there was a long corridor with a golden carpet. Known as the Golden Mile, this is where the majority of the Board Directors had their offices. Their PA had a small office, and once you got through that, you would find yourself in palatial surroundings – nice art, comfy sofas, and a fridge. Always a fridge. A very well-stocked fridge. And the trick we all played was to have late afternoon meetings in a Board Director's office because the fridge would be opened and the free booze would flow.

To be honest, I didn't need to rely on the generosity of Board Directors (not that it is particularly generous to give away booze from a supply that was automatically replenished for them for free). I started out in the Media Department, and the Media Owners all wanted me to spend my clients' budgets with them, so they would take me out to lunch. I'm not exaggerating when I say that I could easily be out to lunch five days a week. And whilst those lunches generally involved really good food in lovely restaurants, they also involved a lot of alcohol. As a trainee, I often tagged along with my Group Head. She was a wonderful, feisty Glaswegian, and next to her, I was a complete rookie in the drinking game. Lunches would typically start off with a G&T (or two) whilst we perused the menu. Then wine with lunch and often some port or a digestif to round things off, particularly towards the end of the week. And after that we'd go back to the office and carry on working (which, in my case, meant spending clients' money on advertising space). The fact that I never overspent a budget is frankly down to luck rather than good judgement, as my judgement was seriously impaired most of the time. But looking back on it, I'm amazed that this was completely normal. No one ever questioned this culture. It was just how we operated.

At another agency, I remember one of my colleagues coming back into the agency after a particularly long and liquid lunch, very much the worse for wear. So much so that the evidence of him having thrown up was clear to see on his shoes. The guys he was with tried to avoid him bumping into the MD who was in the large glass atrium on the ground floor. But my colleague ignored their subtle pleading, and he proceeded to have a fairly incoherent conversation with the MD, slurring his words and stinking of vomit. The MD's response was merely to ask 'Good lunch, was it?' I tell this story purely to indicate how very normal it was for people to get very drunk during working hours – it was completely embedded in the culture of our industry. And it is no wonder that many people who worked in the industry during that time have gone on to develop problems with alcohol in later life.

I left London in the late 1990s, and my last London Agency had a bar in the building. It was known as 'The Gym', so that we could tell our nearest and dearest that we might be late home as we were going to the gym after work. Every time we won a piece of business or won an award, there would be free drinks in the gym. And from memory, there were free drinks every Thursday evening to encourage team spirit and bonding. I spent a lot of time in the gym, far more than I should have in view of the fact that I had two small children at home and a nanny who was waiting for me to take over.

Later in my career, I worked for an agency based in North Devon. Public transport was close to non-existent, so pretty much everyone drove to work, which meant that the lunchtime drinking was very moderate indeed. But despite the restrictions placed on us by our rural location, alcohol still played a part in agency life. Our monthly all-staff meetings included free cans of cider and beer. New starters were taken out to dinner by the CEO and wine would be offered. Team lunches were at the pub, and whoever was paying would have no problem putting the booze through on expenses as well as the food. The team I worked in had a tradition of 'Gin Friday', where one person would bring in a bottle or two of unusual gin, and we would all gather in the boardroom for gin and tonics on a Friday afternoon. In fairness, most people opted for either a very small measure of gin, or plain tonic, but the point is that it raised no eyebrows – never mind the fact that nearly everyone would be driving later that afternoon, never mind that they had work to do. The belief was that getting together over a G&T was fun and good for morale, and therefore good for the business. It is only the pandemic and most people working from home that has put paid to this particular tradition. Gin Friday falls rather flat when most people are choosing to work from home on a Friday these days.

Client entertaining certainly involved good restaurants and fine wines, and continues to do so. And the booze definitely flowed at awards dinners, particularly if we'd won. And when it came to the Christmas party, well, all bets were off. At every agency I worked at, all booze was free at the Christmas party. People seemed to attend with the intention of 'getting their money's worth' and there were some horror stories. One girl was still so drunk the following morning that she wet herself and didn't realize. Another curled up under her desk to catch up on sleep – it was a chilly day so she got very close to the radiator and woke up (or rather, came to) to find she had actually burned her face. And there were several cases of people, how do I put this tactfully, falling asleep in the wrong room or with the wrong person beside them. What is so sad about this is the fact that it seemed normal. The workplace culture quite literally normalized excessive drinking. Worse still, bosses turned a blind eye to some of the unacceptable behaviour that resulted – sexual harassment is fuelled by excessive alcohol consumption, and it is still such an issue in the advertising industry that there is an active movement, TimeTo, backed by the key industry bodies, to try to stamp it out.

These excesses are still going on. Yes, we have made progress, but it is very much a case of 'work in progress' – there remains a great deal still to do. And the organizations that really embrace the change are the ones that stand to gain the most.

In the next two chapters, I will examine the various ways that alcohol could be part of your corporate culture. And at the end of that chapter, there is a link to an online tool you can use to assess the degree to which your business is 'Bottling Up Trouble'.

Chapter summary

- Experiences from my own career which illustrate the extent to which alcohol, and the excesses it can lead to, used to be the norm in the advertising industry.

- Things are gradually changing but the job is far from done.

9

The various ways your business may be Bottling Up Trouble: the bits that are in writing, i.e., policies and contracts of employment

Do you know what your organization's official policy is when it comes to alcohol? Or what your contract says about it? There is of course a big difference between a policy (which is a statement of intent) and something that is enshrined in a legal contract. But how many of us, apart from lawyers, really read every word of our contract? Working for myself, I no longer have a contract, but looking back at previous ones I have filed away, I found that in all of them, the use or misuse of alcohol could constitute gross misconduct, and therefore lead to summary dismissal. Alcohol was specifically mentioned, alongside illegal drugs, as an example of gross misconduct if it should lead to a reduction in my capacity to carry out my duties. But amongst the list of examples of gross misconduct were many examples of poor behaviour, where alcohol was not specifically mentioned, but which are more likely to occur when someone is intoxicated. For example:

- fighting, assault, aggressive behaviour, bullying, or harassment;
- breaches of confidentiality;
- rudeness, insubordination, refusing to follow instructions of a superior;

- negligence or causing damage to property/injury to others;
- failing to follow health and safety rules;
- being absent without permission;
- doing anything which brings the company into disrepute.

There are a number of things in that list that could easily happen when someone was drunk – we all know about violence and aggression as a result of drinking, and if the alcohol has been provided by the employer, or if drinking has been sanctioned by them, it seems a very grey area – is it the employer who is to blame for supplying or condoning the drinking of alcohol? Or is it the employee's fault if something bad happens as a result of them drinking/drinking too much? I really don't think it is clear cut. Telling an employee that they can have *some* of a dangerous, addictive substance, but not too much, is like telling a toddler they can play with a sharp knife but they mustn't hurt themselves or anyone else. It assumes a level of competence and control that is simply not there.

The Company issued a Health and Safety Policy, alongside my contract. but this is all that it said about alcohol:

Employees must be fit to carry out their duties and operate equipment at all times. Employees should not turn up for work under the influence of alcohol, drugs or any other substance which may pose a risk to their own health and safety, the health and safety of others, or damage property or the integrity/reputation of the Company.

At the time when I joined there was no wellbeing policy, although one was introduced while I was there. This encouraged people to seek help if they felt that they were having any mental health issues, but alcohol was not mentioned and nor was there any reference to help that might be provided to someone who was struggling with any form of addiction.

So, the take-out really is 'We'll help you with mental health problems, but not with any issues around dependence on, or addiction to, alcohol, or illegal drugs. Provided that you keep such problems under the radar, we'll turn a blind eye, but if they start affecting your work, you'll be out.' That's not great, is it?!

I got hold of another company's current policy, in which they set out their policy and then answer some likely questions:

XXX's Drugs/substance abuse and alcohol policy

XXX operates a drug-free workplace. We are committed to maintaining a work environment that is free from the influence of illegal drugs (including psychoactive substances, including those formerly known as 'legal highs') or controlled substances. We aim to provide a safe, healthy, and productive workplace for everyone, to prevent accidents, and to comply with legal regulations.

The productivity of our people is our greatest asset, and the adverse effects of alcohol and other drugs create a serious threat to the welfare of fellow employees and clients. While performing your duties or while on our premises, we prohibit the use, possession, sale, conveyance, distribution, or manufacture of illegal drugs, or controlled substances in any amount or in any manner. Any violation of this policy will result in disciplinary action being taken and could result in termination of your employment and/or referral for criminal prosecution. **In addition, the Company prohibits the abuse of alcohol or non-prescription drugs while performing your duties nor while on our premises. If you need help because you have a substance abuse problem, please talk to the People Team.**

What is regarded as unacceptable?

Whilst it is acceptable to drink alcohol in moderation (for example when at lunch with clients), being at work whilst impaired by alcohol is regarded as serious misconduct and will be subject to disciplinary action up to and including dismissal.

What about Company-sponsored gatherings where alcohol is served?

On occasions where XXX sponsor an event where alcohol is served it is up to you, using your best judgement, to decide when you have had enough to drink. The abuse of alcohol, even at a Company-sponsored event, is strictly prohibited.

What if I am off duty and off Company premises?

It is not our intent to monitor or regulate your behaviour off duty and off premises. However, if such off-duty behaviour adversely affects your job performance or brings the Company into disrepute, we reserve the right to take appropriate action.

There is much to comment on in this policy. The first thing is that there is at least an acknowledgement that an employee may have a substance abuse problem, and the implication is that the People Team will help, though I would be much happier if it was made clear that help would be offered! If you want to be cynical about it, that request to 'please talk to the People Team' could simply mean 'please tell them you've got a problem so that they can watch you like a hawk and fire you the minute you step out of line'.

But what follows in this policy reveals a poor understanding of the nature of addiction. The policy states that it is acceptable to drink in moderation, but that being at work whilst impaired by alcohol is regarded as serious misconduct. The first issue is that moderation is extremely difficult to define, but the *real* problem with this policy is that for someone who is dependent or addicted to alcohol, moderation (however you define it) is almost impossible. And the same thing applies to the idea of 'using your best judgement to decide when you have had enough to drink' – that simply reveals zero understanding of what it is like to be addicted to alcohol. Any judgement disappears completely once you have had a drink or two. One of my clients lives in the USA where alcohol bottles carry the suggestion that the purchaser should 'Drink Responsibly', and she told me that every time she saw that, she just wanted to shout 'Don't you think I *would* drink responsibly if I bloody well could? But I can't!'

The legal perspective on contracts of employment and alcohol – UK

Surely, as employers, we can do better than this in the policies we draft and the contracts we issue? This was one of the questions that I put to a solicitor-friend of mine. In a very lawyerly way, he pointed out that he wasn't an employment law expert and had actually had very little experience of alcohol being a problem in the workplace. But he went on to say: 'In terms of what happens in practice, my view is that every case depends on its facts. HR teams are keen to move real disrupters on (and in practice they often do so very effectively without litigation) but where the case is more nuanced and there are allegations or potential allegations of work stress causing the drink problem they will clearly be more caring.' I thought that this was really interesting – he was confirming what I suspected, that HR teams will use problematic drinking as a way of getting rid of people who are 'disruptors'. But if there is a risk that the employee could come back and claim against the organization for putting them under severe stress which led to them drinking, then the case is likely to be looked at much more sensitively.

My next port of call was to talk to someone who specializes in employment law. I was introduced to the super-helpful Karen Bates, from Foot Anstey Solicitors in Exeter. She explained that here in England, disability is one of ten characteristics protected under the Equality Act. The wording is:

A person (P) has a disability if –

a)   *P has a physical or mental impairment, and*
b)   *the impairment has a substantial and long-term adverse effect on P's ability to carry out normal day-to-day activities.*

Having read that, my assumption was that alcohol-dependence would be included as a disability, but I was wrong. There is a clause in the act which specifically states that: *An addiction to alcohol, nicotine or any other substance is to be treated as not amounting to an impairment for the purposes of the Equality Act.*

So here in the UK there is no protection at all for people with alcohol dependence or a history of alcohol dependence. Even though we know that such a dependence will cause long-term physical and mental impairments which *are* covered by the legislation. And in this, Britain is at odds with other English-speaking countries. In Canada, USA, Australia, and New Zealand, the discrimination law does not exclude people with alcohol dependence. A wonderful charity called Alcohol Change here in the UK has questioned the Government on this point and been told that the exclusion exists because alcohol dependence is 'self-induced'. What utter rubbish! As Alcohol Change points out, 'no one chooses to become dependent on alcohol and anyone struggling deserves support without being discriminated against in this way'. The critical point is that addiction to alcohol is *not* a choice. People who are dependent on it need help, not stigmatization. It seems that the UK Government, at the time of writing, is pandering to popular (and misguided) opinion in this approach.

Employees clearly feel that it is not safe to divulge a problem with alcohol. An Alcohol Change UK survey found that 43% of people feel confident their employer would support them if they disclosed a mental health problem, yet only 25% felt the same for an alcohol problem.

If someone loses their job due to alcohol dependence, it can set in train a rapid downward spiral for that individual. Their income is likely to decline or even stop, so that they become reliant on the state. Their health will almost inevitably decline. They may well lose their home. Their relationships are likely to suffer or end. Alone, homeless, and jobless – pretty hard to make a fresh start from there! **Wouldn't it be so much better for everyone (the individual, their employer, the health service, the housing services, the public purse) for that individual to get the help and support that they need as early as possible, so that they can overcome their dependence and put it behind them. And for them to feel hope rather than shame?**

The legal perspective outside the UK

So far in this chapter, I have been considering the situation here in the UK, where I live. But I'm well aware that employment law varies around the world. It simply isn't possible to put together an analysis of the laws, and how they are interpreted, in every country in the world. But I did want to talk about what happens in the main English-speaking countries in the world. I also wanted to share with you how very different things are in France, a country

I know well, having studied the language and spent a lot of time there over the years.

France is well known for its strong culture of protecting the rights of the worker, and a French psychiatrist, Corinne Cabanes, explained that under French law, the employer has a duty of care to their employee that includes the employee's mental health. A French worker who develops a problem with alcohol would be entitled to receive help paid for by their employer. Dismissal would only be a consideration if all reasonable efforts by the employer had been unsuccessful – for example, if the employee either didn't attend counselling or coaching sessions, or refused to engage with them. But provided that the employee made a reasonable effort to overcome their problem, they would not face disciplinary action or the threat of dismissal. However, the stigma around 'alcoholism' is just as strong in France as it is elsewhere, and human nature being what it is, employees with alcohol problems may keep their jobs, but they are likely to find their career progression stalls and that they are (unofficially, of course) branded as 'problem people'.

Canadian employment lawyer Dale Darling also highlighted an issue I hadn't really thought about – it suits employers to 'medicalize' their employees' AUD. If they can get a medical professional to certify that someone is unfit for work due to their AUD, this does two things. First, it distances the employer from any subsequent decisions regarding that employee – they can say it's nothing personal, they are merely acting on medical advice. Second, it strengthens their case should a dismissal be the outcome, and in any subsequent legal action. The medical professional isn't too keen on being used to 'justify' the action of employers, and there is consequently a degree of friction between the two groups. This cannot be healthy.

Chapter summary

- Employees are often only vaguely aware of what their contract of employment says about alcohol, but these documents are vitally important if their drinking becomes a disciplinary issue.

- Whilst not so legally binding, workplace policies are also very important, as they set the tone for the corporate culture.

- Employers should review both contracts and policies to ensure that they are fit for purpose, and that they do not deter employees from seeking the help that they need.

- In the UK, alcohol addiction is deemed by the government to be a lifestyle choice, and it is specifically excluded from the list of protected disabilities under the Equalities Act.

- In most other countries in the world, alcohol addiction is deemed to be a disability and an employee cannot be fired simply because of their AUD, although failing to address the problem or to engage with treatment options offered can lead to dismissal.

10

The unwritten rules that mean you may be Bottling Up Trouble

In this chapter I will highlight a number of subtle and not-so-subtle ways in which the culture of an organization can be favourable to the consumption of alcohol.

Interpretation of policy is often influenced by the job function

Alcohol policy, and how strictly it is enforced, is strongly influenced by what the job actually involves, and alcohol is more likely to be tolerated and/or part of the culture in office-based jobs. When it comes to jobs that involve driving or working with machinery, or interacting with or providing a service to the general public, alcohol during the working day, and even turning up to work with a hangover, are deemed unacceptable. In roles such as these (think delivery driver, teacher, doctor, nurse, shop worker) alcohol is not part of the work-day culture because it would affect people's ability to do their job and could put lives in danger. When someone in one of these roles arrives for work clearly 'the worse for wear', it will generally be noticed and steps will be taken to prevent them from fulfilling their normal role that day, often with fairly dire consequences for their career. The higher profile the role, or the more lives are potentially at risk, the greater the jeopardy. I'm thinking of the significant coverage in 2003–2004 of the story about the Virgin Atlantic pilot who was arrested at Washington Airport as he attempted to take charge of a jumbo jet full of people, whilst under the influence of alcohol. That was a clear breach of the rules by anyone's standards. But the reason that happened is because he had been socializing with his flight deck colleagues during their layover, and didn't pay enough attention to how much he was drinking or to the length of time it would take for the alcohol to be processed. As in so many organizations, the airline had a culture of using alcohol in socializing and bonding. For most people, this was moderate and didn't present a problem, but for this one individual, he wasn't able to be moderate, and he paid a very heavy price, but much less than hundreds of people might have paid if that aeroplane had crashed because he wasn't fit to pilot it safely.

It would be wrong, though, to think that alcohol won't cause a problem in office-based jobs that don't involve piloting an aircraft, operating machinery, or interacting directly with the public or with customers. It does have a detrimental effect on people's ability to do their jobs, as well as on their physical and mental health. People who are under the influence of alcohol at work (or hungover) are likely to display some or all of the following:

- lack of co-ordination;
- slurred speech;
- impaired judgement;
- impaired ability to think clearly;
- erratic or fluctuating emotions;
- impaired memory, both remembering past events and forming new memories;
- slow reaction times;
- nausea and vomiting.

Any of these is going to interfere with an individual's ability to give their best at work. I have worked in an advertising agency where people were occasionally sent home because they were so hungover that they effectively presented a risk to the business by being there in that state. This would typically happen after an awards ceremony where the agency had done particularly well, and the person involved was the 'hero of the hour' and had been bought celebratory drinks by all and sundry. They had done great things for the agency so they were certainly not in danger of any disciplinary action, but after a few minutes of back-slapping and recounting hilarious tales from the night before, the powers that be wanted them out of the way in case they did anything stupid during the day. So, it was really a case of 'out of sight, out of mind'. But of course, we are in very murky waters here. The agency was effectively saying that it is ok to turn up completely incapable of work if you got into that state celebrating winning a big award. But if you were to be drinking with friends who are not in the business, celebrating something that is nothing to do with work, and then turn up unfit for work, that would be a different matter and might lead to disciplinary action. And of course, the long-term, cumulative effects on their physical and mental health will certainly impact their ability to perform well in all areas of their lives.

I don't see the logic of having different policies for different types of job role or different types of organization. Alcohol impairs people's ability to do their job. Full stop.

The language used reflects and shapes the culture

It seems to me that the language used within an organization not only reflects the culture, but it can also shape it. And the reality is that there is still a lot of language in use in and around the workplace that perpetuates the rather extreme drinking cultures of the past. The exact words and phrases will vary from country to country, but it often centres around concepts like 'bonding over a beer', 'I'm buying', 'raising a glass to XYZ'. Phrases like this perpetuate the (unhealthy and unhelpful) status quo.

Western cultures tend to glorify alcohol, to put it on something of a pedestal. It's all around us, in films, on TV, in memes online, on birthday cards. And this happens at work, too. Society (ably supported by the alcohol industry and their marketing teams) tells us that alcohol is *the* way to unwind, relax, celebrate, commiserate, or get to know our colleagues better. As I have already demonstrated, this simply isn't true. Yet we continue to glorify the stuff in the way we talk about it and the roles we give it in business. Those of us in senior roles are in a position to change this, as I will discuss both here and in Chapter 11. And as with any habit change (for that is what we are talking about), the process starts with becoming fully aware of what we are doing at the moment. What jobs are you giving alcohol in your organization? And would you still do that quite so automatically if you knew, with absolute certainty, that it would lead to physical, mental, or emotional pain for some of your employees? Just because things have always been that way, it doesn't mean that's the best way to do things. We used to smoke in the office, and we used to turn a blind eye to sexual harassment, racism, and homophobia. We don't do that anymore.

We should also be aware that language isn't just verbal. What visual imagery is being used in and around the organization? Do invitations to parties feature champagne bottles and corks? What sort of message is that sending out? What about team birthday cards? Do they reinforce the idea that birthdays should be celebrated with alcohol?

When I am coaching, I often suggest that my clients should ask alcohol some difficult questions, and really hold it to account. Business leaders need to be doing that not just in their personal lives, but throughout the organizations that they lead. This is not optional. If you are not part of the solution, you are part of the problem, and you will lose your competitive edge.

Management attitudes

The glorification of alcohol is a societal norm and consequently runs deep in most workplaces. Changing it will take time and inspired leadership. Boards need to walk the walk and to be seen to do so. In my career in advertising, any suggestion that more junior people might want to cut back on their alcohol consumption would have been utter hypocrisy given that Board away-days frequently involved overnight stays and a lot of fine wines over dinner. Indeed, those dinners were one of the main perks of getting onto the Board.

The senior people in an organization are disproportionately influential. Others look up to them and seek to both emulate them and win their approval. Their influence is insidious and below the radar, but it is nonetheless true that the behaviour and attitudes of senior people really do matter. Imagine that it's the morning after a work party, at which a junior member of staff, let's call them Sam, has been noticeably very drunk, stumbling into people and spilling drinks on them before falling asleep/passing out in the toilets. Someone called a cab in order to get Sam home, and there was then a chaotic ten minutes whilst people tried to find out their address – they were far too drunk to remember it. The taxi driver refused to take Sam unless they were accompanied, so one of their colleagues had to go with them. Sam showed up at work the next day very late and very much the worse for wear, and as they walked in, their boss effectively gives them the hero-treatment, 'Ah, here comes the legend that is Sam, who drank the bar dry. Isn't it great that they can't remember their home address, but they know their way to the office? Three cheers for Sam!' I'd love to think that this sort of thing couldn't happen, but I've witnessed similar situations all too often, and the people I spoke to for this book confirmed that such responses are still relatively commonplace. And, honestly, that is not ok. Not only is the boss effectively condoning such behaviour, but I would argue that they are actually encouraging it. Interestingly, there does seem to be something of a gender divide here. Bosses are likely to be older, and many of them have different standards for men and women. Behaviour that will earn a man the label of being a 'good lad' may well be seen as over the top or unacceptable for a woman. But, important as it is, the issue of gender politics in the workplace is a separate subject.

I want to be clear about what I see as being wrong with the boss's behaviour here:

- They are glorifying alcohol – by deeming Sam to be a 'legend' because of their drunken antics, they are giving out the message that that is what it takes to win their (the boss's) approval.

- They are encouraging excessive drinking that could lead to Sam developing a dependence on alcohol.

- They are making light of the potentially dangerous situation that Sam got themself into. Passing out in a toilet, not knowing your own address and being incapable of getting yourself safely home are all extremely risky. I feel a complete and utter hypocrite writing that, because there were certainly occasions when I was too drunk to get myself home safely. I was lucky. Nothing really bad happened. But it is better not to rely on luck.

- The boss is condoning the fact that Sam has shown up at work incapable of doing a proper day's work – that is not good for the business and could be very serious if Sam makes a mistake or is rude to a client during the course of the day.

- They are condoning the fact that Sam's drunken behaviour the night before will have spoiled other people's enjoyment of the evening (just to remind you, they bumped into people, spilled drinks on them, had to be rescued from the toilets where they had passed out, needed to have people find out where they lived and had to be accompanied home in a taxi).

- The boss does not necessarily know the whole story of the evening. Would Sam still be deemed to be a 'legend' if they had gone on to assault someone later that evening?

- Their approval may make other employees feel that is how to get the boss's attention and approval. If they are non-drinkers, this could be demotivating, making them feel like outsiders. Or it may encourage people to drink when they otherwise wouldn't have drunk or wouldn't have drunk so much.

- Condoning Sam's behaviour is sending out a tacit message that this is an acceptable way to behave. Those who feel otherwise will be made to feel out of place and are likely to be open to offers of employment with organizations where standards of behaviour are more in line with their personal values.

In Chapters 11 and 12, I will suggest how different attitudes from senior management could have a profound impact throughout the organization in a relatively short period of time.

The role of alcohol at work events

The tone of work events is very much set by the attitudes of the most senior people attending those events. Expectations can be set well in advance – the boss who tells the new trainees all the hilarious tales of carnage and bad behaviour at last year's party is encouraging similar behaviour this year. That isn't helpful. Those who like a drink will seize the opportunity to get drunk at the company's expense (for the expectation is very much that alcohol will be supplied free of charge and in unlimited quantities). Career-damaging behaviour may well result. Meanwhile, those whose attitude to alcohol and drunkenness is more ambivalent are likely to get the impression that this event is not for them, and they may stay away. If this happens, the organization is failing to bring everyone together – they are dividing rather than uniting.

So, what are the work events which typically involve alcohol? The most obvious work event which involves alcohol, and probably the most universal, is the annual party which is most commonly held around Christmas/New Year. I'm happy to say that the days of unlimited free booze do seem to be numbered. I know I may sound a bit of a killjoy saying this, but I do see it as morally wrong to position free alcohol as a treat or reward, and to supply it in unlimited quantities to people who may not be used to it, knowing what disastrous consequences may result. It is also wrong to suggest that it is necessary for people to drink alcohol to bond with each other and have a good time. And if you don't believe me, go and watch a group of five- or six-year-olds in a playground.

Now I am not saying that there should be no alcohol at all at a work party. But what I am saying is that it shouldn't be centre stage and the thing that everyone is focused on. If there is free alcohol, it should be limited to one or two drinks, but that can be difficult to supervise with drinkers being adept at securing non-drinkers' 'rations'. In my view it is better if all alcohol is paid for, but all non-alcoholic drinks are free. And I would very much discourage you from buying alcoholic drinks for your teams or putting your credit card behind the bar. In the same way, I would want to ban the practice whereby you host a pre-party party in your hotel room, to 'get everyone in the mood'. It sends out all the wrong messages.

The drunken office party can cause serious harm to those who drink to excess. It can also lead to sober-shaming[21] of those who steer clear of the booze. What sort of a world have we created, where sober-shaming is even a 'thing'?

If all of this sounds the death knell for the 'traditional' office party, then so be it. Heavy drinking and good business just don't mix. There are many other ways to bring people together, thank them for their hard work, celebrate success, and strengthen relationships.

Alcohol isn't just a feature of the workplace culture once a year at the big party. It crops up far more regularly than that, as I examine in the rest of this chapter.

Rewards and incentives

What role does alcohol play in the way that you reward and incentivize your staff? Are you reinforcing cultural norms and putting alcohol on a pedestal, giving the message to your staff that alcohol has an intrinsic role to play in the highs and lows of day-to-day life? These cultural norms include champagne to celebrate achievement or wine as part of a 'pamper-hamper'. Let me give you some examples that I encountered during my career or which people have told me about. See how many of them might apply to your organization.

- A book publisher is unable to attend a successful author's book launch party, but sends them a bottle of very expensive vintage champagne instead.

---

[21] https://alcoholchange.org.uk/get-involved/campaigns/stopsobershaming; www.theguardian.com/lifeandstyle/2021/oct/05/keep-up-the-pub-invites-and-dont-sober-shame-how-to-support-a-friend-to-stop-drinking

- An employee gets engaged and the employer sends them a congratulatory bottle of champagne.

- That employee then gets another bottle (or maybe a case of champagne or fine wine) when they get married.

- And (extraordinarily) more champagne arrives on the birth of a baby, to a breast-feeding mother. Really? Yes, really!

- New business wins, promotions, winning awards, or other notable achievements are acknowledged with gifts of champagne or wine.

- A lawyer I know won a high-profile case and was sent a case of extremely expensive vintage champagne by their grateful client – that lawyer has been sober for over a decade and attends at least three AA meetings a week. She put the champagne into a charity auction.

- Champagne to mark length of service, and retirement.

- Christmas gifts of alcohol to staff or suppliers – during my time in advertising I would say that the ratio of booze to other gifts (such as chocolate or flowers) was about ten to one. And that carried on, even after I had stopped drinking, which goes to show that a bottle of champagne is almost a default business gift. Little or no thought goes into it.

You'll notice a bit of a theme in that list – champagne. It has been very cleverly marketed for decades and is now as closely associated with celebration as diamonds are with love (also a marketing construct, by the way). And this association of alcohol with celebration goes back a long way, thousands of years in fact.

Alcohol has long been associated with special events. According to researchers at Penn University,[22] the earliest known alcoholic beverage was a mixed fermented drink of rice, honey, and hawthorn fruit and/or grape. Residues from the beverage, dated

---

[22] www.pnas.org/doi/10.1073/pnas.0407921102

7000–6600 BC, were recovered from early pottery from Jiahu, a Neolithic Village in the Yellow River Valley in Northern China. The researchers state that these fermented beverages were of considerable social, religious, and medical significance. They explain how fermented drinks have marked major life events, from birth to death, as well as victories, auspicious events, harvests, etc. They also highlight how 'upper-class' individuals with leisure and resources 'were drawn to feasting on a grand scale, which often features special fermented beverages served in and drunk from special vessels. In their most developed form, such celebrations were formalized into secular or religious ceremonies for the society at large.' So, alcohol has been part of human ritual and celebrations for around 9,000 years.

The story of the wedding at Cana in the Bible has Jesus turning water into wine because the wine had run out. It was clearly entirely normal to serve wine at a celebration such as a wedding, and in our modern Western culture, this Bible story is often used to justify alcohol and its role in celebrations. Indeed, it can be used as an argument against teetotalism. But I would argue (and apologies to any devout Christians reading this), that in transforming the water into wine Jesus actually did mankind a disservice. The Jesus that I know would not knowingly have performed a miracle in order to encourage people to drink something that is highly addictive to human beings and capable of causing unimaginable pain and suffering. Nor would he want this miracle to be used as an anti-temperance argument. It's just my opinion, but I named my coaching business 'Wine to Water Coaching' because, to me, ditching the booze in favour of water is the true miracle.

But I am lapsed Catholic who rarely darkens the doors of a church, so I thought it would be a good idea to check out the significance of the wedding at Cana with some people who know what they are talking about. Huge thanks to Reverend Anne Heywood and Reverend Nigel Done for their time and insight. The first thing they did was to correct me when I referred to the wedding at Cana as a miracle. It is actually a Sign. St John (the only one of the gospel writers to mention this story) was big on Signs – he mentions seven of them in his gospel, and they are all pointing to the ultimate transformation that Jesus offers mankind. So, this is a story about transformation, and it is full of symbols. A wedding symbolizes the end of waiting and possibility, hope, and transformation. The water is a symbol of ritual, and biblical scholars see it as representing anything and everything that corrupts us and prevents us from living a full life. It is significant that there are only six jars and not seven, as would have been expected – another sign of incompleteness. The point of the story is that anything that is tainted or incomplete can be transformed by Jesus. The wine is a symbol of spiritual sustenance. It is also important to note that Jesus is pretty secretive about what he is doing. He's not interested in winning people over by ensuring there's a huge amount of wine to drink at a wedding reception. It's not about the wine. Both of my expert witnesses said that it would be completely wrong to interpret this story as pro-alcohol or anti-teetotalism.

Pub culture and bonding with colleagues

A major feature of working life for many people is the culture of drinking together with colleagues after work. Here in the UK, that is often at the pub, but elsewhere in the world, it will generally involve going to a bar. For the sake of ease, I will refer to it as 'pub culture'. And I think that there are three levels of potential harm attached to pub culture.

Employee-organized and employee-funded

The first, and least harmful, level is where a group of colleagues organize between themselves to go out and socialize together. This will typically be in an evening, or at a weekend, and given the prevailing culture, it is very likely to involve going somewhere where alcohol is available. Depending on the people involved, alcohol may be central to their plans, or it may be incidental. But the motivation will be either to get to know each other a bit better or to just enjoy each other's company and/or to enjoy a shared interest. Even if alcohol is a key factor in the planning, the event would not be happening if the individuals did not want to spend their free time together with some of their colleagues. The event will tend to cement friendships and, as such, it will almost definitely be beneficial to you as their employer. Importantly, the individuals attending will be paying out of their own pockets, and this is an important point, as it *can* serve to put a natural brake on excessive alcohol consumption. This isn't always the case, but it is an important differentiator between this self-organized and self-funded type of event and those that are funded by you as the employer.

Boss takes their team out for bonding drinks

In this scenario, the boss almost definitely means well when they suggest any off-site gathering that could involve alcohol. Let's imagine that a manager speaks to a new trainee and says 'A group of us are going to the pub after work this evening. Would you like to join us? It would be a good opportunity for you to get to know everyone a bit over a few beers. I'm buying.' That manager probably thinks they're being a good boss, human, friendly, thoughtful, approachable, inclusive, and welcoming.

But let's look at it from the perspective of the trainee. Let's imagine that she has a long-standing commitment to babysit for her sister that night. Or she has children of her own to get home to. Or she's the only female in the team and she feels uncomfortable going out with a group of men she doesn't know very well. Or she's newly pregnant or trying to get pregnant and doesn't want to drink alcohol. Or she doesn't drink alcohol for religious reasons. Or she's previously had a problem with alcohol and is in the early stages of recovery. Or she just doesn't like drinking alcohol. Or she's had a bad experience of being harassed by colleagues after they've had a few drinks. Or she has a review meeting the next day and wants to be on top form for it. I hope you can see that if any of these were true, she would be in an uncomfortable position. If she doesn't go, she'll feel that she is excluding herself from the group and may be seen as unfriendly or stand-offish. She may also feel that she is putting herself at a disadvantage in comparison to other trainees who may attend. They will be getting to know the boss and the team and she won't, and this could impact her career development down the line.

This may seem far-fetched, but I know, from the interviews that I've conducted for this book, that it really isn't. There are many professions where being a 'good fit' or a 'good team player' is one of the criteria for career progression, and there are a lot of organizations, particularly in the legal and management consultancy worlds, where only a proportion of trainees will be offered full-time contracts. These people will feel under intense pressure to take part in anything that their boss suggests and to 'play the game'. So, they feel a degree of compulsion to attend even if they would rather not. They are disempowered and that is never a good feeling.

And then when our young trainee gets to the pub, she may find it difficult to say she wants a non-alcoholic drink. She doesn't want to be seen as boring or a 'lightweight'. Now it really doesn't matter if anyone actually says this to her, it's about what she fears that others might think. We are in the world of perception rather than reality, and her perception may well be that she should have an alcoholic drink if she wants to fit in. So, she has a drink.

- Scenario one is that she has just one drink. And she gets home fine having had a really nice evening, no harm done.

- Scenario two is that she has a few drinks and realizes she's now vulnerable, so has to spend money on a taxi, and the following day she wakes up with a hangover. No serious harm done, but she's a bit worse off financially, and she doesn't feel great.

- Scenario three is that she has way too much to drink and, not being used to alcohol, she is sick at the pub and has to be taken home by a colleague. She is too ill to go to work the next day as she effectively has alcohol poisoning, and she spends the weekend terrified that she may lose her job, or at the very least, have permanently tarred her reputation. Not a great outcome, I'm sure you'll agree. And almost definitely not what her boss intended.

Of course, there is another potential outcome, which is that she goes, has a lot to drink, but suffers no serious ill-effects. Indeed, everyone is a bit groggy the next morning at work, and there is a lot of banter about the events of the previous evening and she feels one of the team, an insider and not an outsider. Sounds great doesn't it? Until I tell you that, this is the start of her developing a habit of drinking heavily with her colleagues. At the time, it all seems harmless, but years down the line, she looks back and sees that this is when her dependence on alcohol started. That was certainly what happened to me and to countless of the clients I have coached. I'm not blaming anyone for the difficulties I got into, but there are certainly some line managers and bosses who aided and abetted me.

Alcohol is available on site, either free or at subsidized rates

The most harmful form of workplace 'pub culture' is when the pub or bar is actually on site, within the workplace, and particularly if the alcohol is free or cheaper than elsewhere.

In my analysis, I draw a distinction between the hospitality industry, where serving alcohol is an intrinsic part of the business they are in, and other industries where the availability of alcohol would not be considered essential to the core purpose of the business.

There are many documented cases of people in the hospitality industry developing AUD, and we have seen an example of this in Chapter 3. It can be difficult to determine cause and effect here. Is it the case that working within the industry and being exposed to alcohol on a daily basis serves to normalize drinking, and accelerates the development of AUD? Or is it the case that those with a tendency towards drinking more than is good for them are attracted to working in the hospitality industry precisely because of the ready availability of alcohol? In truth it is probably a bit of both. But regardless of the cause-and-effect argument, employers in the sector have a particularly important duty of care towards their employees, and indeed towards their customers. When it comes to customers, here in the UK, it is actually illegal for a bartender to serve alcohol to a customer who is clearly inebriated, and they and their employer can be fined for doing so, and the establishment may lose its licence to sell alcohol. It seems clear to me that this law is anything but vigorously enforced, but it does serve to help bar staff prevent some excessively drunken behaviour.

But what about protection for staff who work with alcohol every day, whether in the hospitality industry or in the manufacture and distribution of alcohol? Many employers do try to do the right thing, and we saw in Chapter 3 that the Marriott Del Mar Hotel had set limits on the free alcohol to be served at their Christmas party – just two drinks and no spirits. But the bartender who went on to kill another driver in a road accident later that night ignored these rules. It is a sad fact of life that rules will always be broken and occasionally there will be tragic results. That is not a reason not to have the rules. They are needed, and it is important that they are in place and well communicated – not just what the rules are but *why* they are in place. Just as important as the rules, though, are the twin pillars of education and culture. And we will discuss both of these in Chapters 11, 12, and 13.

Let's turn our attention away from the hospitality and alcohol-manufacture industries and look at the effects of having a bar in the workplace. It is not so long ago that police stations in this country had bars and indeed the police station in Grimsby had a bar (The Peelers Retreat) as recently as 2018, although my source tells me it wasn't open all that time. There are scores of tales of inebriated senior officers being driven home in squad cars by their junior officers after a session in the 'police club' in the station in times gone by – hardly good use of public funds! It would be lovely to think that these in-station bars were closed because of a significant culture change, but it appears that cost-cutting was the key factor. And talking to serving police officers now, it seems that there is still a long way to go before the boozy culture is eradicated. And one of the most concerning things is that so many serving police officers say they drink at the end of their shift in order to relax and unwind after a stressful day. I am part of a group of coaches who work, pro bono, with various police forces and other blue-light services to help increase awareness of the fact that alcohol exacerbates stress and anxiety. We are making great progress, but there is a lot of work still to do!

Working in the emergency services is, of course, stressful work. But they are not the only sectors to have a culture of workplace drinking.

When I was working in advertising in London, virtually every agency had a bar, and it was often free. But that was a long time ago. I tapped into my network of contacts, and, more usefully, my daughter's, to find out how much things had changed. Things are definitely not as boozy as they were in my day, but there are still agencies with a free bar every evening from 5–8pm. And the thing that has made the biggest difference is the pandemic and the proportion of people working from home. Sadly, some leadership teams are using the free bar as a reason to come back to the office. Interestingly, some agencies pointed out that they had alcohol brands as clients, which put them in a 'difficult' position. I get that – but as the great advertising man Bill Bernbach famously said, 'It's not a principle until it costs you money.'

Perhaps advertising agencies are unusual though. I decided to research the reality of a couple of other industries with reputations for a workplace drinking culture, and found that the picture in insurance, the legal profession, and management consultancy was much the same as advertising. I believe that this is because these are all jobs where evaluating the supplier's output is somewhat subjective, so the suppliers schmooze their clients to cement relationships.

Drinking whilst actually doing the job

To many people, the idea that others might be drinking alcohol at their desks may seem quite ridiculous. I thought it was a thing of the past, but it is still going on, and I fear it may have actually increased as a result of the pandemic and working from home becoming more prevalent.

You've probably seen funny memes about the fact that everyone on the zoom call thinks I've got coffee in this mug but it's actually a G&T, or advice to blow on your wine to make people think it is tea or coffee. And they are funny. But believe me, as a coach, I have worked with many people for whom this became a reality during Covid. And they found it a really difficult habit to break, which is unsurprising, given the addictive nature of alcohol. So here we are talking about drinking at the desk that is being done in secret, with shame and guilt, and it is definitely not sanctioned by the employer. Indeed, you would find it very difficult to know what is going on in the privacy of your employee's own home. The only way you are likely to find out is if the employee (or possibly a member of their family) speaks up and asks for help. And as we've already discussed, that is highly unlikely to happen. Or the other way that the employer may realize what is going on is if the employee is visibly or audibly under the influence. I have heard of this happening a couple of times in informal, internal meetings, late in the evening. And in those cases, no disciplinary action was taken. Indeed, the employees concerned argued that work was intruding into their off-duty time, and they were under no compulsion to even attend the online meeting. The fact that they did so with a beer in hand or slightly under the influence is seen as neither here nor there. And the line between work time and leisure time became very blurred during the pandemic, and to an extent, it has remained so. I suspect that there is a fair bit of hidden desk-drinking going on when people are working from home. The sad thing is that when it gets to be a problem, people are too ashamed to ask for the help they need. This is one of the things that I hope this book will change.

But the surreptitious tipple at home whilst on a work Zoom call is only part of the story. There is another form of drinking at the desk, and that is what goes on actually in the office and is sanctioned by the employer. It happens in organizations which have a workplace bar. An employee can go to the bar and get a drink, then return to their desk with it – and they will probably earn a few brownie points for going back to their desk and continuing to work. In the last London agency I worked in, this is something I did quite often. I'd go to the bar for half an hour or so, unwind and have a chat to a few people, and then take a drink or two back to my desk whilst I continued to work in what was effectively my free time. The way I saw it was that if I had gone home at 5.30, I would be sitting at my kitchen table with a glass of wine and getting on with my work, so it was fine to be drinking at my desk in the office. Now in my case, my desk-drinking only took place in the evenings, and I suspect that this is generally the case for many people. However, this does raise a couple of issues.

First, there is the issue of work/life balance. If evening work is routinely required, that says to me that one of two things are going on. It may be that the individual is getting distracted during the working day and having to make up for lost time in the evening, in which case it is up to their line manager to spot what is going on and work with them to get more done during the working day, so that they can get home on time. Or it may be that the individual's workload is too great, in which case their line manager needs to escalate this and find a solution. Of course, there will be the odd period where extra work is needed (pitches, for example) but if this becomes commonplace, and if people are making it more tolerable by drinking at their desk, then it is a problem that needs to be addressed. Failure to do so really is tantamount to bottling up trouble.

The other issue is that when people are drinking, they will not be doing their best work. I know that novelists like Ernest Hemingway claimed that alcohol increased their creativity, but Julia Cameron's 'The Artist's Way', which is something of a manual for creativity, was only written once she had got (and stayed) sober. And recent research studies by the University of Essex and Berlin's Humboldt University[23] have indeed corroborated her anecdotal evidence – alcohol does not improve creativity, and nor do most drugs. And for those of us who do not work at the cutting edge of creativity, there is certainly no case to be made that we will do our best work when inebriated. Indeed, we have already seen that alcohol reduces our mental capabilities and is likely to lead to mistakes and poor decision-making.

---

[23] www.theguardian.com/science/2023/mar/24/drugs-and-alcohol-do-not-make-you-more-creative-research-finds#:~:text=Yet%20researchers%20have%20found%20this,training%20programmes%20are%20more%20effective

Drinking whilst governing the country

Drinking on the job leads to impaired performance. And that is why I (and many others) found it very troubling to read the reports into what was going on in 10 Downing Street during the pandemic. You will remember that staff parties were being held in Downing Street, during a period when we (in the UK) were all being told to stay at home and not mix with anyone who wasn't a member of our household. There were tales of junior members of staff being sent to the supermarket to buy booze, and returning with suitcases full. The investigation into whether or not there had been illegal parties had to deal, first, with the fact that there was something of an evening drinking culture in 10 Downing Street. A Government source was allegedly quoted as saying: 'The Number 10 press guys routinely drink at their desks on a Friday evening... that goes on for hours, but [they are] still fielding calls and emails.' Someone else talked about the 'usual scene of press guys having drinks at their desks with a small group of No. 10 staffers'. And on at least one occasion, the then Prime Minister, Boris Johnson, joined them. This is the heart of Government we are talking about, during an unprecedented national crisis. And they were, quite literally, drinking on the job.

The drinking culture within Westminster may account for some of the frankly unfathomable decisions that have been made there over the years. But it is also responsible for some totally unacceptable behaviour. In what felt to me a bit of a 'no sh*t Sherlock' moment, Parliament's behaviour watchdog, the Independent Complaints and Grievance Scheme (ICGS), reported in October 2023 that[24] 'a culture of drinking is fuelling inappropriate behaviour in Westminster'. That inappropriate behaviour includes predatory sexual advances, groping, sexual harassment, shouting, and swearing. The report also highlights that alcohol affected the ability of many witnesses to recollect incidents.

---

[24] www.bbc.co.uk/news/uk-politics-67137917

A report published in Business Insider in March 2022[25] discussed the hidden drinking problem in Parliament, and raised a number of very interesting points which reinforced to me the necessity for this book. The article suggested that:

- MPs are drinking because of the stress the job, the long and anti-social hours, and the loneliness of being away from home for most of the week.

- Alcohol is being used as an alternative to getting the help needed to address mental health problems.

- The ready availability of alcohol on site makes it all-too-easy to drink regularly and excessively – there are eight bars in the Palace of Westminster, all serving cheap alcohol.

- It is relatively common for MPs to be inebriated when voting.

- MPs are afraid to seek help because of shame or for fear that the information will be used against them and that they will be punished rather than helped. There is a widespread feeling that Parliament isn't a safe place for anyone to seek help.

Richard Piper, Chief Executive of Alcohol Change UK, said he felt that the 'combination of long working hours, plus high accessibility, plus an old boys' drinking culture' was a 'really toxic mix'. He went on to say that the solutions did not lie in blaming the individual, but in tackling the culture. **'It's like if you have a fish tank and the fish keep dying but you never change the water. What we have in Westminster is dirty water.'**

I would argue that the dirty water is not limited to Westminster. Our culture is soaked in alcohol, and we urgently need to change that culture. And that change will not come about by vilifying those who develop AUD, leading to others being fearful of the consequences of asking for help. It will come about by helping

---

[25] www.businessinsider.com/the-hidden-drinking-problem-in-uk-parliament-2022–3?r=US&IR=T

people to realize that developing AUD is *not* a result of a defect or moral failure in the individual. It is not their fault, and it can (and does) happen to absolutely anyone. And with the right help, anyone and everyone is able to put this firmly behind them. **We need to shift our cultural response to AUD from condemnation to compassion.**

Networking

Networking is a key part of business life. Having a strong network of contacts is considered to be a huge asset and, from our earliest days in our working lives, we are encouraged to build up our network.

One way we build our network involves approaching strangers/ virtual strangers at industry events and striking up conversations. Back in the day, the end goal was to swap business cards with them. These days it is about getting to the stage where you can be confident that they'll accept your LinkedIn request. For anyone who is a natural introvert, this can be deeply uncomfortable. Our instincts are to exercise caution with strangers, and yet, if we are to successfully climb the career ladder, we are required to engage complete strangers in conversation. And even if we are lucky enough to be introduced to people, we still need to shine sufficiently that they will remember us and want to connect with us. And that is where alcohol comes in. It is pretty much guaranteed to be a feature of every networking event that happens after midday, and many a delegate at a conference has used a drink or two to give them the 'Dutch courage' to go and speak to someone important. But it can backfire:

- Alcohol adversely affects our cognitive abilities (our ability to think clearly), and if either party in a conversation has been drinking, this will serve to 'dumb down' the conversation and make it less memorable – hardly the best way to make a good impression.
  - The would-be networker may have too much to drink before they get to speak to the important person they want to connect with, so that the impression they

create is unfavourable. They may be remembered but for the wrong reasons.

- ○ The important person they want to speak to may have overindulged, meaning that they probably won't remember the interaction.

- What starts out as moderate drinking at a networking event may turn into going on somewhere else to continue the conversation over another drink or three, resulting in a hangover and a loss of productivity the next day.

- And for both parties, routine drinking at these events may contribute, over time, to developing a dependence on alcohol.

But there are ways to network without alcohol being involved. Breakfast events are great, and I absolutely love the speed-dating style events where you get just five minutes to have a brief chat with someone before moving on to the next person. Whether online or in person, these are a great way to establish contact and know whether it is worth following up or not.

The other form of networking is where staff deliberately strengthen their relationships with contacts as a way of ensuring that they will be able to call in a favour at a future date. One political insider said that:

> [Alcohol] is definitely used as a medication for the insanity of the job, for sure. So much networking is still done via informal drinking. Often you actually can go a whole day without doing any work and then get a week's worth of networking done in one night at the [nearby pub] Red Lion.

We are human beings and have an in-built need for connection with others. Getting to know the people we deal with, whether they are colleagues, clients, or suppliers, makes for better working relationships. Things become less transactional and more human. When we have got to know someone a bit, we are more likely to do them a favour, more likely to have a fruitful and mutually beneficial 'give-to-get' negotiation with them. In my early days in advertising, I worked in the media department, responsible for planning and buying where ads would appear. As such, the media-owners were suppliers who were keen to build good working relationships with me. A lot of wine was drunk, and at the time, I thought this was great. But it became a problem down the line. And for some people, it is a problem at the time.

Entertaining

Entertaining clients sounds like a real perk, but for some it can be a curse. If you are someone who knows that they already have a degree of AUD, you may seek to avoid client entertaining because you know how risky it can be. You know, intellectually, that you don't want to drink. But your subconscious has other ideas. You know, intellectually, that you need to limit yourself to one or two drinks or you risk embarrassing yourself. But after one or two drinks, your judgement is impaired and all manner of unplanned consequences can result. And these can have a detrimental effect on your career.

Let me tell you the tale of one of my coaching clients – let's call her Sue. (This account is retold with her permission, but I've changed one or two small details to protect her identity.) Sue told me about the time when she was expected at a client dinner. The entire client team had come to town, which was something of a rarity. And Sue's company had arranged a fairly lavish dinner for both teams to really get to know each other. Now Sue had been battling with AUD for a while. She was white knuckling it, relying on the dual tactics of willpower and avoiding being anywhere near alcohol. She clearly did not want to go to the dinner. So, she spoke to her manager. Fearing that she would hinder her career progression if she told the truth, she made up an excuse about childcare. Her manager simply told her to get it sorted, as this was an important event. Sue *really* didn't want to go as she simply didn't trust herself around alcohol. So, she went to see one of the Mental Health First Aiders within the company – wracked with shame and embarrassment, she explained the situation, and was treated with kindness and compassion by her colleague who promised to speak to the manager on her behalf, without divulging any confidential details. But the manager remained completely intransigent. Sue needed to be at the dinner and her absence would be a black mark against her. So, Sue had to go. She was terrified that she would drink, and even tried, unsuccessfully, to get hold of some Antabuse (a drug that makes you very sick if you drink after taking it). She went to the dinner, and got through the pre-dinner drinks without any alcohol, but at the senior client's insistence, had a glass of wine with the meal. And that one glass turned into two, which turned into many, many more. She became extremely intoxicated and doesn't really remember how the evening ended. What she does remember, all too well, is that her behaviour became an HR issue the following morning. Sue asked the Mental Health First Aider she had spoken to to accompany her to the HR disciplinary meeting where she had to defend herself from summary dismissal for bringing the company into disrepute. Thanks to the Mental Health First Aider's support, Sue kept her job. But her 'guilty secret' was now something that HR knew about. Sue felt that her career there was over. She moved on quite quickly. She also became a client of mine at around this time, and after a period of us working together, she was able to put alcohol firmly behind her. She is now joyfully alcohol-free and is doing phenomenally well in her new job. And despite the stigma, she is contemplating going public with the story of her struggles with AUD, so that she can help others. So, there is a happy outcome to this story. What is less good news, though, is that her former employers still haven't changed anything in their policies, so the next 'Sue' to be put in that situation will face the same Hobson's choice – don't go to the dinner and jeopardize his or her career development, or do go, and risk dismissal if he or she drinks too much. Employers really must do better than this!

Expense accounts and alcohol

Are there any businesses that allow employees to expense their cocaine? Or their heroin? Or their ecstasy? Well, no, obviously not, because they are illegal. What about other legal but harmful substances then? Like cigarettes or vapes? Again, the answer is no. And yet, it is completely routine for bosses to sign off expense claims that include alcohol, or are entirely for alcohol. This is crazy.

Alcohol being expensable is perpetuating its normalization in society. And that is not a good thing. Employers are effectively gifting their employees a substance which is addictive and damaging to their physical and mental health. And it's harmful to the business as well, and can lead to inappropriate behaviour, and worse. As I say, it's madness.

Let's look at a couple of examples. Earlier in this chapter, we looked at the pub culture/after work drinks which is still prevalent in so many organizations. This is frequently funded by a team leader or manager who buys the drinks and claims them back on expenses. I was quite excited when someone from a London ad agency told me that it was very difficult for them to expense team drinks, until he went on to say that the agency he worked at had a bar which was open every day from 5–8pm and where drinks were always free. So, there is no need to take the team out for drinks when unlimited booze is freely available (literally, freely) in the agency every day of the week. This is a financially motivated policy, nothing at all to do with employee wellbeing.

What about business lunches and client entertaining? Well, in my research I did come across some organizations where alcohol could not be claimed if the lunch was just between employees, and it does seem that this is a growing trend, which is fantastic. But it is an altogether different picture when it comes to client entertaining. If a client wants to drink, the supplier supplies the booze, and will be under an obligation (implicit or explicit) not to make the client feel uncomfortable about the fact that they are drinking alcohol. The supplier needs to make it feel normal, and totally acceptable. And generally, that means 'keeping them company', and staying out with them until they are ready to go back to the office or back home or to their hotel room. Of course, it is possible for someone either to explain that they aren't drinking or can't drink, but often they don't want to have to explain. I have a lawyer friend who had many pregnancies which resulted in miscarriages – this was deeply personal stuff, and not something she wanted to discuss with clients in order to explain away the fact that she wasn't drinking. The culture of clients expecting to be 'wined and dined' makes people like my friend feel uncomfortable, and that is wrong. I believe that is a far greater wrong than the client who might feel uncomfortable about drinking alone. And be under no illusion, there are lots and lots of people like my friend out there, all with their own reasons for not wanting to drink.

The bottom line is that the routine availability of free booze on expenses contributes to people's descent into the pain and misery of AUD. We have to do better than that, surely?

I have developed an online tool which will help you assess the alcohol culture of your organization, and will highlight areas that may need work. My intention is that this should be the start of a conversation within your organization, a way of raising awareness and encouraging action. Inevitably, an online tool such as this can only scratch the surface, and if you find there are areas of your business that need attention, I would urge you dig deeper, using external and impartial researchers to ascertain the scale of the problem.

Here is the link to the Building Up Trouble interactive online assessment tool:

www.bottlinguptrouble.com

Chapter summary

All of the following are areas where the 'unwritten rules' in a business can shape its culture regarding alcohol:

- How policies are interpreted (and how this varies by job function).

- The language used (words and images can glorify alcohol, which is very unhelpful).

- Management attitudes can be very influential, and can, in some cases, leave non-drinkers feeling marginalized.

- Work events often revolve around alcohol (and often end badly for individuals).

- Using alcohol to reward and incentivize staff or as a gift shows a lack of imagination and can sometimes be wholly inappropriate.

- The custom of going to the pub or bar together is often held up to be a good thing as it encourages staff to bond – however, it is frequently counter-productive and can set people up for a lifetime of addiction. There are better ways of bringing people together.

- Drinking at the desk happens all too easily when there is a bar within the office – and if people are working late, in their own time, the employer really can't say anything. The issue may well be excessive demands being made of the employee.

- Drinking whilst governing the country is clearly a bad idea, but is definitely a feature of British politics.

- Networking events can be something of a trial for some people, particularly those who are natural introverts. But using alcohol as a social lubricant is not a strategy for success.

- Client entertaining may sound glamorous but can be a real difficulty for anyone with AUD. Employers need to be much more sensitive.

- Allowing employees to put alcohol on expenses encourages them to drink, and this cannot be in their best interests, nor the employer's.

11

Road map for changing your workplace culture around alcohol

So far in this book, I have been discussing the ways in which alcohol is holding business back, and I hope that by now, you are thinking about areas of your workplace culture where there might be room for improvement. The rest of this book will focus on how you can make the changes that are going to get you ahead of your competition, be that commercially and/or as an employer-of-choice with a loyal and motivated workforce.

It can be difficult to make meaningful changes within an organization, but Change Management Theory provides a good blueprint. First, a quick reminder of the key principles:

1. Awareness of the need for change – the start point of the process is to recognize that there is a need to shift from the current state of play.
2. Clarity about what success looks like – set clear, attainable goals and know how you will measure success.
3. Desire to participate in and support the change – generate buy-in and enthusiasm amongst everyone involved.
4. Knowledge of how to change – providing the necessary tools, training, and resources.
5. Ability to implement the required skills and behaviours – ensuring that everyone understands and can execute their role in the change process.

6.   Reinforcement to sustain the change – regular feedback, rewards, and recognition.

I'm now going to break this down into a series of steps which business leaders can follow.

Step 1 – Assessment

The business management textbooks will tell you that you need to understand the current situation, the reasons for change, and the potential impact of the change. This is much easier when others have tried this before, but we are talking about breaking some new ground here. Up until now, alcohol has been given something of a free pass in business, so we are talking about a fairly major culture shift. How do you conduct an objective assessment of the alcohol culture in your organization when it isn't something you've really thought about before, and for which you have no bench-marking data? Well, luckily, I have done a lot of the work for you. I have put together the interactive Bottling Up Trouble assessment tool, which you can complete for free from my website: https://bottlinguptrouble.com.

Completing the Bottling Up Trouble assessment tool will furnish you with a list of areas for consideration, recommended priorities, and a suggested timescale for implementing the changes.

Step 2 – Planning

Once you know your priorities, you can start to develop a vision for the changes you want to implement. At this stage, I would like to point out that there are a couple of imperatives:

- You will need a very senior person to act as sponsor for this project. I will go into detail on the leadership role later in this chapter – it is a crucial role, and without someone filling it, the change is unlikely to happen, and highly unlikely to endure.

- You will also need a small but committed team to champion the project. They should work with the nominated sponsor to map out the plan in detail, identify key milestones, and the resources that will be needed. Importantly, they should also identify any potential obstacles (human or otherwise). Forewarned is forearmed! I will suggest how you can recruit this team in order to ensure that they work well together and achieve their objectives.

Step 3 – Communication

In a sense, communication isn't really a step, as it is an essential at every stage. With any significant change, it is really important that everyone involved understands the reasons behind the change, the potential benefits, and how they personally will be impacted. Over the last year or so, many businesses have sought to get their employees to return to the office after the Covid years where they were predominantly working from home. Some organizations have managed this very well, and others have, frankly, made a complete hash of it, leaving staff feeling resentful and unappreciated. Be under no illusions. These changes will be very beneficial to your organization, but there will be some people who are highly resistant. We have seen that alcohol is very embedded in Western culture, and there will be many members of staff who see it as their right to mix alcohol and work, and there will also be others who already have a degree of AUD, who may feel very threatened by the changes. Sensitive and non-judgemental communication will definitely be required. It will also be important that employees see that the loss of the perceived perk of alcohol at work is more than offset by a range of attractive new benefits targeted at mental and physical wellbeing.

Step 4 – Training and support

This is the make-happen piece in the programme of change. The team will need to provide the necessary tools, resources, and training in order to embed the culture change. Education will be a key plank in this, as will the sensitive provision of support for anyone who is already suffering from any level of AUD. Particular attention should be paid to ensuring that the Board and Senior Leadership Team fully embrace the changes that are proposed. Divisions will quickly become apparent and would risk the entire project being derailed – hence the need for an extremely senior sponsor.

Step 5 – Launch and implement

This is when the rubber hits the road, when you launch the programme of changes. Success will depend on this being treated as a top priority by the most senior people in the organization. Top-down commitment will engender enthusiasm and buy-in. And the senior team, alongside the project team, will need to monitor both progress and sentiment, and agree what adjustments may be necessary. It will be really important to be seen to listen and adapt, whilst not deviating from the overall intent.

Step 6 – Review and reinforce

Each organization will have to decide on the best way of reviewing the progress they are making. Larger organizations are likely to have regular staff surveys in place already, and it would be sensible to use these, particularly as they are often conducted by external agencies, thus providing employees with confidence as regards confidentiality. It is really important to share positive news both internally and externally. So if, for example, the percentage of people responding positively to a question about feeling listened to goes up, this would be a good message for internal communications (posters, intranet, staff portal) and external communications (email signatures, client newsletters, social media posts, trade press interviews).

The importance of the sponsor

The role of the sponsor is critical. They need to be a very senior leader within the organization as they need to have the authority, influence, people skills, and resources to drive and support the change. Their enthusiasm should be unquestionable, and they need to have real credibility within the organization. When employees see very senior people backing a project, they are much more likely to take it seriously. It is crucial that the rest of the

Senior Leadership Team are fully supportive of the vision and of the sponsor, and that the necessary resources are made available without question. Any boardroom bickering or penny-pinching will quickly become public knowledge and could undermine the project. Equally, the Board need to support the project delivery team by ensuring that they have the time and manpower to embed the changes.

Ideally the sponsor should be prepared to make it personal, to share their own story or their own motivation for making the change of culture such a priority. It may be that they themselves have had a struggle with alcohol. If so, them sharing this would be incredibly powerful. It would say all the things that need to be said:

- This organization does not believe that a history of difficulties with alcohol is in any way a barrier to career progression.

- It is entirely possible to put difficulties with alcohol behind you and to go on to have a successful career.

- The sponsor is there to support and champion anyone in the organization who is struggling with AUD.

- Developing a problem with alcohol can happen to absolutely anyone and should never be a source of shame or stigma.

- Sharing a deeply personal story makes the sponsor very relatable and breaks down the them-and-us barriers that can exist between senior leaders and their employees.

In her book *Atlas of the Heart*, renowned American academic and researcher Brené Brown says that 'vulnerability is the birthplace of innovation, creativity, and change', and it is so true. The leader who makes themself vulnerable by sharing their own troubled history with alcohol will earn considerable respect from colleagues of all levels, and will be playing a significant part in facilitating change and in helping to prevent others from suffering the same fate in the future.

However, it is definitely not essential for the sponsor to have had difficulties with alcohol either personally or amongst their friends or family. Strong leaders are not just good businesspeople. They also have good interpersonal skills and plenty of empathy. And they can bring all of these to the fore when they advocate for a change in the organization's attitude to alcohol. With no personal axe to grind, they are able to bring a degree of objectivity to proceedings.

Although it is best practice to have a single (and very senior) individual leading the change programme, that individual should ideally have very visible support from the rest of the Board or Senior Leadership Team. In reality, it is likely that most Boards will have more than one person who has, or has had, an unhealthy relationship with alcohol. Even in smaller organizations where this might not be the case, leaders are likely to know of people who have had problematic relationships with alcohol. But, this is still a taboo subject. People tend not to talk about it, and indeed, they may not really even admit it to themselves if they, or someone they know, has a problem. Denial is alive and well in the world of AUD. So, I recommend that the leadership team should all complete the AUD assessment that you will find in the Appendix.

People may answer 'yes' to more than one of those questions, but still feel very reluctant to 'go public', and this is very understandable. Society has made alcohol into the social lubricant par excellence, but any degree of dependence on it is seen as unacceptable and a source of shame and stigma. So, it is entirely natural that people feel ashamed to admit how much they drink or that they might have a problem. It can feel deeply hypocritical to be publicly calling for a change to the corporate culture around alcohol whilst simultaneously drinking at work functions or hiding a few drinking skeletons in the closet. But unless we do something to help people overcome this burden of shame and stigma, we will never get out of the rut that we are in. We need to start somewhere, and my recommendation is to start at the top. I encourage everyone who sits on a Board or has the title of Manager to reflect on their own alcohol use. If it feels somewhat out of control, that is not something to beat yourself up over. You can actively demonstrate this culture change in action, get the help that you need, and then share your story so that those below you in the hierarchy know it is safe for them to do the same thing. Get a coach to work with the board, both collectively and individually, to work through the answers to the questions below and the cognitive dissonance that is likely to come up. Obviously, I have to declare an interest here, as I am a certified coach who works with individuals and companies. But the key thing is that it works. And the question you should ask yourself is 'Can we, as an organization, afford not to do this?' And if you personally have any degree of AUD, 'How much better and happier could my life be without alcohol being in control?'

Of course, not all Board members will have issues with alcohol. But they may still be part of the problem, displaying a lack of awareness and sensitivity. The sort of questions that a coach would explore with them might include:

- What does alcoholism or AUD conjure up for you?

- Do you have a friend or family member who has had a problem with AUD?

- Or, are you aware of a tragic story of someone who did not get the help that they needed and maybe lost their job/ home/marriage or even their life because of their AUD?

- Are you aware of anyone in your organization who might have AUD?

- Are you aware of anyone in your organization who may be using alcohol to self-medicate for stress or anxiety?

- Are you aware of anyone in your organization who doesn't drink and who might feel uncomfortable about the drinking culture? Could their views be shared (publicly or anonymously)?

- What other cultural norms have changed within the company in the past, and what can be learned from how those changes were implemented?

- Are there people within the organization who have made significant lifestyle changes who might be happy to talk about how they made those changes (e.g., getting fit, losing weight, stopping smoking, becoming a vegetarian or vegan, taking up yoga or meditation)?

The importance of an amnesty

Implementing a major culture change is a big deal. And for it to be effective, everyone in the organization needs to feel completely safe. If there is any fear of reprisals for past actions, people are not going to engage, and you'll find that there are small groups of cynics and nay-sayers threatening to derail the project. The best way to reassure people that this change is significant is for there to be a very well publicized amnesty right across the organization.

This means that the message has to come out loud and clear and repeatedly, from the very top of the organization, and it must be reinforced by managers at every level. The precise messages that should be communicated will vary according to what has been agreed within the organization's Charter for Change (see the next section), but will include the following:

- What is changing?
- Why is it changing?
- The benefits of the changes.
- Expectations going forward.
- Timescales – changes should ideally be immediate but accept that it will take time for new culture to bed in.
- Acknowledgement of how big a change this is, for everyone, management included.
- Focus is entirely forward-looking.
- Guarantee that everything that is in the past will stay there.
- How to play your part.
- Who to go to with questions or suggestions.

The key part of any amnesty is that it truly is an amnesty – everything that is in the past has to remain in the past.

When I worked in advertising, we used to develop brand manifestos for clients, and they were incredibly useful documents, referred back to time and again as they were the distillation of all the key information about the brand's position and strategy.

I recommend that every organization that commits to changing their culture around alcohol should develop their version of a culture manifesto. I think of this as the 'Charter for Change', but you can of course call it what you like. The important thing is that it is a landmark moment in the organization's cultural history, a real turning point. It will take a lot of internal consultation before you are able to draw it up and agree it, and that process will be made easier by using an external consultant to guide you (again, I have to declare an interest here, but most businesses are already used to working with external consultants, so you probably won't take too much convincing).

Once your Charter for Change has Board approval, it needs a big razzmatazz launch (without alcohol!) and to be unmissable throughout the organization. It should shared (electronically and physically) with every single person, at every level, full and part time, permanent and temporary, and in every far-flung outpost. Leave no stone unturned or communications opportunity unused. This activity should be reinforced through every available media channel, internally and externally (e.g., website, intranet, workplace posters, screensavers, email signatures, internal and external newsletters, relevant merchandise). Depending on the size of your organization, you may already have an internal comms team who will be well equipped to deliver this. If not, an external consultant will be able to work with your team to deliver a memorable and exciting launch campaign.

What are the key components for a Charter for Change?

The background – what has led to this?

- The problem you are solving.
- An overview of the change, in a single sentence (the elevator pitch).
- Details of the change(s).
- Benefits of the changes.

Here is an example I have drafted for a hypothetical client – a London-based advertising agency which currently has a higher-than-average turnover of young women employees. Exit interviews have revealed that many of these young women feel that they 'don't fit in' with the agency's culture. The agency has an in-house bar and a reputation for throwing lavish parties.

Charter for Change (example)

Every so often, a business needs to look at the way it does things and ask if there is room for improvement. We have been doing that in our 'You speak, we listen' project over the last six months, and are grateful to everyone who gave us such valuable feedback. We have learned a lot about ourselves and about the realities of life for many of you. We have been saddened to realize that some really good people have left us because they didn't feel comfortable within the culture that has developed within the company.

Society's attitudes change and it is essential for an organization like ours to stay abreast of societal changes. Attitudes to race, gender, age, sexuality, disability, and religion have changed and are reflected in the blind recruitment policies we now have in place. However, we have come to understand that our policies and practices around alcohol need to change. Alcohol will no longer be a part of our workplace culture.

Alcohol is harmful to the mental health of those who drink it, even in relatively small amounts, as it contributes to stress, anxiety, and depression. It also leads to a number of serious health risks. It is therefore inappropriate for us to be supplying it, and to be setting expectations that you will drink it. Alcohol is highly addictive, and it seems completely wrong that we should blame and shame individuals who have become addicted to a substance that we actively encouraged them to drink. Alcohol addiction is progressive and can happen to absolutely anyone. It should not be a source of shame, and it will not be one within this organization.

Alcohol education will now form a key plank of our wellbeing programme, paying particular attention to the dangers of using it to self-medicate for stress. The new programme will help everyone develop more effective and healthier stress-management strategies.

We will provide effective help for anyone who feels that they already have, or are developing an unhealthy relationship with alcohol, and we pledge that asking for help will be seen as a positive and not a negative for that individual. In order to kick-start the process of de-stigmatizing problematic drinking, and to give you confidence that we really will not sit in judgement of anyone, each member of the Board and each Manager will be open and honest about their relationship with alcohol, including what help they are getting and what changes they are making. We are committed to this and will make it a particular focus during Alcohol Awareness Week, when we plan to make it the theme of all of our internal and external communications.

We strongly believe that no employee should ever feel that they are expected to drink alcohol in order to progress in their career. Managers taking their team out to bond over a beer or two in the pub may seem innocuous, but our consultation has revealed that it can actually be very divisive and leave people feeling excluded. Therefore, it will no longer be possible to put alcohol on expenses for any internal meetings or team sessions, or for any meals when away from home.

We are committed to developing strong relationships within the business and to developing and funding a range of 'bonding' activities that do not involve the consumption of alcohol. The first of these will be to replace the free bar on Thursday evenings with a fabulous and delicious free lunch every Thursday. The time will be automatically blocked out in everyone's diaries, and everyone will be encouraged to eat together.

We will no longer encourage and facilitate the consumption of alcohol. We will not serve alcohol on the premises and nor will it be given to staff, clients, or suppliers as a gift. Instead, we will encourage a more personal and meaningful approach to gifting, supporting a range of small businesses in the process.

We will write to all of our clients to explain that, for the benefit of everyone who works for us and with us, we are changing our culture around alcohol, and we will ask for their co-operation. We do not believe that it is appropriate for anyone to be drinking at lunchtimes, and so it will no longer be possible to submit claims for alcohol at lunchtimes with clients. Some alcohol at client dinners will still be permissible, but wherever possible, employees are asked to consider alternative forms of client entertainment, that do not involve alcohol.

There will be a change of emphasis at parties, with a focus on getting to know people. We have asked the social committee to suggest alternatives to the team, departmental, and company-wide parties we have done in the past. Whilst no free alcohol will be served at any parties, all food and non-alcoholic drinks will continue to be free.

Finally, but importantly, we will be reviewing contracts of employment, to reflect these new policies. Everyone who wants to will be offered the chance to sign an addendum to their existing contract, reflecting the company's judgement-free stance, and our commitment to offering effective help to anyone who feels that their relationship with alcohol has become problematic.

All of these changes will make a positive difference not just to each of us as individuals, but to our ability to hire and retain the best people. They will also boost our productivity and profitability. We believe that everyone who works here should share in that productivity bonus. We will therefore allocate 10% of annual profits to a mental health fund, to be used for our employees' choice of initiatives. The only stipulation is that the initiative should be beneficial to anyone who chooses to take part, for example, a constant supply of fresh fruit in the office, and regular fitness, yoga and meditation classes.

Chapter summary

- It is really important to set and communicate your intentions, and using the Change Management process is a very helpful framework:
  - assessment;
  - planning;
  - communication;
  - training and support;
  - launch and implementation;
  - review and reinforce.

- It is vital that you have a respected, senior figure within the organization to act as sponsor and champion for the changes you are making.

- It is also very important to put an amnesty in place, so that people feel completely safe in coming forward with suggestions or requests for help.

- A Charter for Change will ensure that the message is disseminated across the organization and can be referred to as often as is needed.

12

Implementation of the No BUTs Road Map: short-term imperatives

Leaders need to lead

Changing the culture of an organization is a challenge, particularly in the face of some strong emotional attachment to, and possibly some physical dependence on, the subject of the change. But there is no getting away from it, alcohol is harmful to business, and harmful to the individuals who work for the business. A leader who genuinely cares about the people in their charge has to recognize the need to create a workplace culture which neither encourages nor facilitates consumption of alcohol. Simon Sinek, author of the best-selling book *Start With Why*, says 'Leadership is not about being in charge. It is about taking care of those in your charge.'

The American leadership guru Warren Bennis, author of *On Becoming a Leader*, said 'Leadership is the capacity to translate vision into reality.' The vision we are talking about here is one where alcohol has no role in the workplace, where no one feels they need to drink alcohol to fit in or to progress in their career, where all employees are aware of the impact that alcohol can have on their physical, mental, and emotional wellbeing, and where anyone who feels they may be developing a problem with alcohol is able to get the help that they need, through their employer, without being stigmatized.

Translating that vision into reality requires inspirational leadership. The leader needs to make sure that the rest of the senior team have fully bought into the vision. All change involves some degree of risk, and the task of a leader is to help those around him to focus on the upside of the change (whilst he or she minimizes the risk). But the reality is that, in this case, the risk really isn't that great:

- The changes are already happening in society anyway. Here in the UK, the latest NHS data (for 2022) indicate that 42% of young women aged 16–24 do not drink alcohol/have not drunk alcohol in the last 12 months (and the same is true for 34% of young men).[26] These figures have been steadily increasing and have doubled since 2011. Just stop and think about this – more than four in ten young women aged 24 or under either never drink alcohol or have not done so in the last 12 months. This is a choice they have made about how they want to live their lives. And one of the key factors in that decision is the impact that alcohol has on mental health, with 53% of UK 18–34-year-olds saying they are concerned about the impact of alcohol on their emotional wellbeing (versus 40% of 35–54s and 17% of over 55s).[27] Providing a workplace environment where these young people feel comfortable is going to give you the best chance of retaining this talent. And as these young people progress in their careers, alcohol is going to become increasingly anachronistic in the workplace. The businesses that change their culture now are simply ahead of the curve, with all the business advantages that accrue from that.

- You may have some employees who feel strongly that they should be able to drink alcohol during the working day and/or at the company's expense. They might even leave because of your new policies, rather than take up your judgement-free offer of coaching to help them develop a healthier relationship with alcohol. That would be sad for

---

[26] Source: Health Survey for England, 2021.
[27] Source: Kantar Profiles/Mintel, April 2023.

those individuals, but you have to ask whether they are really the employees you most want to retain.

- There is the potential impact on client relationships to think about too. It is extremely unlikely that clients would be overt in giving the lack of free alcohol as a reason for changing supplier. However, it is definitely true that business relationships are strengthened by socializing, and historically a lot of that has happened in bars and restaurants. And it still can, just without the booze (certainly at lunchtime, and preferably at dinner too). The growth in really good alcohol-free brands mean that the non-drinker is no longer forced to nurse a glass of tap water.

But the real issue is not about risk but about doing the right thing. We know that alcohol is harmful physically and to the mental and emotional wellbeing of those who drink it. As responsible employers, we should be doing what we can to ensure that everyone who works for us fully understands this, and in particular that they have alternative strategies for dealing with the stress and anxiety that characterize 21st-century life. Some healthy alcohol-free ways of building client relationships include taking some form of exercise together, like yoga, pilates, a gym class, a run, or an afternoon's hiking. These activities offer plenty of opportunity for people to really get to know each other. They are also good for both physical and mental health, and that is more than can be said for a boozy lunch. Encouraging a workplace culture that promotes the consumption of alcohol is, quite simply, morally wrong. And it is even more wrong to then shame and vilify those who become addicted to the very substance we have encouraged them to drink.

I believe that HR teams, and those who lead these teams, have a vitally important role to play in changing our corporate cultures around alcohol. They will be responsible for setting the tone of the conversations, for drafting and implementing the new policies, for overseeing new contracts, and for ensuring that those who need help with AUD get the support that they need.

I want to look at each of these areas in a bit more detail, but I am aware that I am not an expert, and that there will be significant differences in both legal frameworks and customs in different countries. Therefore, I will stick to general principles.

HR leadership

During my career in advertising, I have come across some wonderful HR Directors with high emotional intelligence (EQ), who make everyone feel valued. And I've come across others who are more interested in process than people, are full of distrust, and apparently pre-programmed to say 'no' to any request. It is those with high EQ and a genuine interest in their fellow human beings who will succeed in changing the culture of an organization. These changes cannot be imposed from on high; they need to be 'sold' to the organization, and that is where strong and effective HR leadership comes in.

It is important that HR leaders have an innate interest in psychology, in what makes people tick, and have their finger on the pulse of changes in society. Provided that your HR leaders meet these criteria, they should buy into the rationale behind changing the culture around alcohol. That buy-in is all-important. The head of HR will be a key person to support the overall champion/sponsor of the change. And, of course, they may actually be the sponsor, the driving force, in which case they will need the wholehearted support of their senior colleagues on the commercial and operational sides of the business.

The role of HR teams in changing the alcohol culture

- Assessment of status quo – much of the assessment of the status quo will need to be conducted by the HR team. Or, if the assessment is being done with the help of a consultant, the HR team will be the primary point of contact for that consultant.

- Consultation with staff – part of the Bottling Up Trouble assessment is to ascertain the views of staff, and this is likely to become a task for HR teams. They should ensure that staff understand the purpose, are confident about confidentiality, and are free from fear about any judgement. In other words, staff need to have full confidence in the HR team's integrity.

- Communication of what is happening, and why, will be vital at every stage of the process, and so excellent communication skills will be needed. Effective internal communications require good strategic thinking and excellent planning, so the HR team need to embody these as well.

- Drafting new policies will be part of the HR team's responsibilities, and this requires sensitivity as well as attention to detail, and the ability to plan and organize.

- Legal knowledge – it will be important for someone in the HR team either to have a good understanding of the legal perspective, or to be able to work effectively with an external legal advisor. This will be particularly important when it comes to drafting new contracts of employment. In most countries, changing an employee's contract of employment after they have joined can be a tricky business. However, in this case, the changes will be favourable to the employee – previous contracts may have threatened dismissal to anyone becoming addicted to alcohol, whereas the new contracts will focus on supporting those individuals, with dismissal only a last resort. Being drunk at work has never really been permitted, so there won't be a change in that regard.

- Implementing training/education programmes may fall within HR's remit, but I have assumed that it will actually be done by wellbeing teams, and I will cover this in the next section.

- The HR team will certainly have overall responsibility for ensuring that anyone suffering with AUD gets appropriate support and help, and this is also covered later in this chapter.

- Finally, the HR team are likely to have budget responsibility for developing and implementing the changes, so someone on the team will need to take responsibility for setting a budget, securing it, and ensuring it is adhered to.

Stress-management: the wider role of HR in breaking down a pro-alcohol culture

Stress relief is one of the most commonly cited reasons for drinking, and of course, not all of that stress will be work-related. But much of it will, and there is a great deal that the HR team can do to prevent that stress from occurring in the first place, and equipping people with healthier stress-management strategies.

What exactly do we mean by stress? Stress is a natural reaction that your body experiences when you perceive a threat or feel overwhelmed by the demands of a situation. It's your body's way of preparing to deal with challenges. It isn't inherently harmful, and if you think about the stress you might feel before delivering a major presentation, that surge of adrenalin can actually be helpful in ensuring that you prepare and rehearse properly. Short bursts of manageable levels of stress aren't a problem – it's when the degree of stress is acute (i.e., really high), and/or chronic (i.e., sustained over a long period of time) that it becomes harmful.

Stress harms us in a number of ways:

- Physically:
  - increased heart rate and blood pressure;
  - muscle tension and aches;
  - digestive issues;
  - headaches;
  - sleep problems.

- Mentally/emotionally:
  - anxiety;
  - irritability;
  - mood swings;
  - depression;
  - reduced motivation;
  - difficulty concentrating;
  - burnout.

Looking at this list, it seems something of a no-brainer for you as an employer to minimize stress for your employees, and to give them good stress management advice. And a good place to start is for you, and particularly those in HR, to be aware of the factors that contribute to stress in the workplace.

Here are the key stress factors in the workplace. In every case, HR teams can play a role in minimizing these stresses, mainly by facilitating open communication.

Workload – heavy workloads, tight deadlines, a requirement to work beyond normal working hours, and excessive job demands can be highly stressful. HR teams should be monitoring the hours that people are working, but accurate monitoring can be very difficult, particularly for senior people, or when people are working from home and/or taking work home with them in the evening. And of course, a large part of the problem is that when people are very stressed, they find they can't stop thinking about work, even when they want to. So it is not just a question of monitoring hours worked, but asking people how they are *feeling* about their workload, and how it is impacting them (mood, sleep, relationships, diet, exercise, etc.), and what they are doing to try to manage their stress levels. Regular staff surveys are an excellent way of doing this, but is also important that managers are trained to spot signs of stress in their teams, and that everyone feels able to raise issues. A recent survey by the UK's advertising charity NABS (National Advertising Benevolent Society)[28] revealed some alarming statistics. It said that 71% of people felt that the advertising

---

[28] NABS All Ears Report, October 2023.

industry needs to pay more attention to mental wellness and 35% still don't feel they can talk about mental wellness. The report acknowledged that many managers were promoted, potentially too early, because of a very tight labour market and because of their ability to do the job, i.e., their craft skills or technical ability, rather than their people skills. The report concluded that managers need to be better trained in the human aspects of management.

That same report from NABS also highlighted that it is not enough to have a good policy – there needs to be genuine commitment to following through on that policy and ensuring that there is a forum for continuous dialogue:

> The actions of leaders in the workplace can make a big and positive difference to their teams' mental wellness. Leaders can do more to ensure accountability, and to ensure the support is in place to close the gap between intention and real-life experience... The industry needs to put increased focus on ensuring that there is an ongoing dialogue that enables every voice in the industry around mental wellness to be heard, recognized, and addressed.

Good managers will be aware when their team is under intense workload pressure, and will ensure that this is acknowledged and that they are able to take some time off after the particularly intense period is over. It is a sad truth that HR teams can sometimes be a bit 'jobsworth' about this, insisting that forms are filled in and correct procedures followed. When this happens, managers simply by-pass them, and the recognition and time-off-in-lieu compensation is awarded on the quiet. Much better for HR to trust the managers in the business to do the right thing by their teams, and not get too involved beyond monitoring what is happening. That way they can ensure that things are being done reasonably fairly, and that appropriate action is taken if the workload pressure is consistently falling on the same few people.

Job insecurity is another major contributor to stress, whether that be about job stability or the fears of layoffs. HR teams can remind the business leaders of how easily rumours can start, and how destabilizing this can be. They should ensure that there is good and early communication if there is a need for layoffs or redundancies, so that people know exactly what is happening and why, and what the processes will be. Being open and honest is really important, and it is also a good idea to avoid dragging the process out as it inevitably becomes a distraction. Clearly there needs to be an appropriate consultation period, and in unionized industries, this can mean a lengthy process. But it is often the case that unions will co-operate with employers who intend to be more generous than is required by law. It goes without saying that HR teams should fully understand the legal position and have good relationships with the unions.

Lack of control – feeling that you have very little control over your work or the decisions that affect your job can be very stressful. I encountered this once during a merger. I moved from having an office that I shared with just one person, to being in an enormous and very noisy open-plan office. The ceilings were high, the floor was wooden, and there was no sound absorption at all. My job involved a lot of thinking, and I simply couldn't think straight in this gigantic room of about 50 noisy people. I used to sneak back to my old office to work, and if challenged, I said I'd come to pick up some files that had been left behind. That was a relatively minor thing, and when I raised it at a management meeting, we realized that it was an issue for lots of people, and sorted things out pretty quickly. But I was lucky, because I was reasonably senior and am pretty capable when it comes to advocating for myself. There are many employees who feel powerless over their working conditions and are suffering high levels of stress as a result.

One of the most common areas where people feel a lack of control is over their working hours, and this is an area where HR can make a real difference. Giving people flexibility over their working hours, and indeed place of work, can make a massive difference. Allowing parents to structure their working day around their family commitments or to work from home more during school holidays means that those employees are able to strike a much better balance between work and home life. Pre-pandemic, there was a prevailing attitude that working from home was really a pseudonym for swinging the lead, and it was generally accompanied by extravagant air quotes. But the pandemic positively changed all that. It proved that it is entirely possible for people to be extremely productive whilst working from home. One business I spoke to told me that although only a third of their staff were remote workers, that group accounted for just over half of all 'employee of the month' awards, and they felt that was because those people were really grateful for the opportunity to work in this way.

There will be some businesses or organizations where flexibility is more difficult, and where people are required to work at a specific location. But if HR's response to requests is more 'let's see what we can do' and less 'no, that's not how it works round here', it will be better for employees' stress levels and better for the organization's productivity.

Most organizations now have a wellbeing team, and they have a unique and incredibly important role. They are generally volunteers from across the organization who have undertaken some level of mental health first aid training. They are people-people and have nothing to do with the disciplinary processes that are undertaken by the HR team. Importantly, they are seen as 'safe' people to talk to. A member of staff who is worried about something can talk to a member of the wellbeing team in confidence, knowing that what they say will go no further.

But the role of the wellness team goes beyond triage and first aid. They can set the agenda for the organization, and without doubt one of the biggest challenges at the moment is striking the best balance between working from home and being in the office. Bear with me – this is connected to alcohol.

We are social beings, and it is important for employers to consider how to bring employees together in ways that do not include alcohol. It is particularly important to consider how difficult it is to socialize and make friends when working remotely, especially for those who are new to an organization. Microsoft conducted some research in 2022, and saw that new hires who worked remotely developed smaller networks within the organization, and were effectively disadvantaged.[29] My son is a software engineer, so I was particularly interested to read the research that indicated that software engineers who were new hires struggled to ask for help when working remotely (due to the isolation between teammates, scheduling difficulties, the lack of corridor conversations, etc.), and they communicated with fewer people overall compared to those who joined pre-pandemic. This matters from an alcohol point of view because we saw in the pandemic that when people feel lonely and isolated, they are more likely to turn to alcohol. And if they are working remotely, it is, of course, much harder for the employer to pick up on the problems that are developing.

The Mental Health charity, Mind, here in the UK, estimates that 15% of the workforce are going through some form of mental health problem at any one time, and most of those problems are depression, anxiety, and stress, all of which are known to be exacerbated by alcohol, if not actually caused by it. The charity advises that 'talking is a healthy way to unburden difficult feelings', and they go on to suggest:

> if you want to cut back on alcohol, avoid situations where you may feel tempted to drink. If you usually socialize over a drink, give some thought to other activities you could enjoy with friends or distract yourself from having one drink after another by playing darts or pool or taking to the dance floor. If your friends understand what you're aiming to achieve, they'll be less likely to badger you to keep drinking.

This is perfectly sound advice, if a little superficial. But what if the pressure to drink is coming from your employer, rather than your friends? That is much harder! And that is where the wellbeing team come in.

---

[29] www.microsoft.com/en-us/research/uploads/prod/2023/03/Large-Scale-Analysis-of-New-Employee-Network-Dynamics.pdf

The role of the wellbeing team

The wellbeing team should be drawn from across the business and not tied to the HR function. As such, they can be the ones to call people out on the pressure they might, possibly unwittingly, be putting on others to drink. They can set the tone as regards being more open and talking about feelings. They can lead small meetings and training sessions, where people are encouraged to open up. They can share resources and their own stories. They are the ears and eyes of the organization, and are aware of the stresses that they and their colleagues are under.

Here are just a few of wellbeing team initiatives I've been made aware of as I spoke to people whilst doing my research for this book:

- Organizing workshops and training sessions to raise awareness about mental health issues, reduce stigma, and provide employees with tools to manage their mental health effectively.

- Organizing stress management workshops (and, in my opinion, these should definitely address the fact that alcohol is widely considered to be a way of managing stress, when in fact it makes it worse). Helping people access stress-reduction programmes such as mindfulness, yoga, meditation, and relaxation techniques.

- Creating a (physical) library of helpful books that can be borrowed by anyone who may be struggling with their mental health.

- Creating an online portal of wellbeing resources such as podcasts, videos, articles, book recommendations, worksheets, as well as information about local mindfulness, meditation, yoga, and fitness classes.

- Creating a 'time-out' room with comfortable furniture and a no-laptop policy, where people can sit and chat/listen to music/de-compress.

- Instigating a regular 'look after yourself' time each month. The last ad agency I worked at, Bray Leino, instigated

'Wellness Wednesday'. Once a month, the office closed at lunchtime on a Wednesday, and we all put on our 'Out of Office' messages, and were encouraged to do something purely for the pleasure of it. For me, that meant getting my walking boots on (and usually my wet weather gear too), and heading out onto Dartmoor with friends and colleagues for a few hours. Others would curl up by the fire with a good book. Or go to a yoga class, unencumbered by small children. Or do some cooking. Or some gardening. Or visit a friend. We didn't have to account for our time, but I'm pretty sure that we all benefited from it and the company did too.

- Creating a learning fund whereby anyone who wants to take a course or learn a new skill can apply to have it fully or partially funded. Some organizations allocate a certain amount of money to each employee, to be spent in this way. My daughter-in-law works for a management consultancy who offer this, and she used hers to learn sign language. Someone else I know learned pottery and has now developed this into a reasonably lucrative side-hustle.

- Establishing links with and discounts/subsidized membership at local gyms and fitness centres to encourage people to take more exercise. The link between physical health and mental health is well-established.

- Setting up a course in managing your finances – here in the UK, we have been going through a pretty grim cost-of-living crisis, and one wellbeing team funded an expert to run an online course which people could take anonymously at a time to suit them. The expert was also available for one-on-one sessions with anyone who needed advice – and the employer picked up the bill.

- Working with the company's Board to establish a hardship fund, so that if an employee's circumstances changed dramatically, they would be able to cover their mortgage or rent in the short term. The examples I was told about included helping a young father of three whose wife tragically died aged just 38. They had life insurance, but whilst everything was being sorted out, he knew he didn't need to worry about money. In another case, an employee's mother had a serious stroke whilst on holiday in New Zealand and the hardship fund paid for her to fly to be with her mother. More common are the cases where people's mortgage repayments have sky-rocketed and they were able to meet the repayments whilst also getting free financial advice about how best to manage their situation – advice that was paid for by the employer.

- Organizing wellness challenges that encourage employees to engage in physical activities, healthy eating, or stress management, with appropriate incentives for participation (e.g., free cinema or theatre tickets, or a basket of fruit).

- Running a regular staff survey to assess employee satisfaction and wellbeing, and use the feedback to make informed decisions about future wellbeing initiatives.

- Improving the environment at work – better lighting, improved décor, plants, and a decent coffee machine.

- Providing subsidized or free lunches, ideally encouraging people to eat together in order to strengthen interpersonal relationships.

- Putting free fruit in the office – this was another thing that Bray Leino used to do. It was cut during a lean period for the business and everyone missed it so much! As soon as funds permitted, it was back – and I have it on good authority that the takings in the sweet-and-crisp machine rose significantly during the no-fruit period and then dropped back again as soon as the fruit bowls were reinstated. A healthy outcome!

You can see that the wellbeing team have a big role to play in making the workplace a healthier and more pleasant environment, and in educating their colleagues about stress and stress management. But in my view, their most important role is to provide a truly safe place for employees to learn about alcohol, discuss their issues, and get the help they need. The wellbeing team will need to fulfil this role until such time as there remains no hint of stigma around AUD, and until all employees have full confidence that talking to the HR team about any aspects of their AUD would not in any way threaten their job or career progression. And that will take a little while. So, the wellbeing team is absolutely at the heart of achieving the culture-change that is needed.

A continuous process

I suspect that there are remarkably few businesses in the Western world where not a single employee has a problem with alcohol. Even if alcohol is not a part of the workplace culture, it is ingrained in our social fabric, and this inevitably leads to AUD in some people, and if they are drinking regularly and/or heavily when they are not at work, that will start to have an impact on their performance at work and on their mental health.

You may be reading this, as a business leader, and reassuring yourself that it is not an issue in your business – you may even be at home with a glass of wine in hand as you read this, as you tell yourself that you are pretty sure that no one in your organization has a problem. My challenge to you is 'How would you know?' You can be the most approachable boss of all time – the stigma around alcohol dependence is still huge, and people are simply not going to divulge that they have an alcohol problem to the boss. Even in countries where the law would prevent them from being dismissed for this (and sadly, the UK is not one of those countries), they will still fear that their reputation will be tarnished, and that they will become, as one person said, 'a marked man', and that they will be passed over for promotion. For anyone dealing with an alcohol problem that is impacting their ability to do their job, their default is likely to be to keep their head down and hope that no one notices. And a lot of bosses don't notice, or are they simply turning a blind eye because their own drinking habits mean that this would be a rather uncomfortable topic of conversation?

It really doesn't matter. This isn't about apportioning blame. This is about how we change the culture, so that people feel genuinely safe in talking about their problems, knowing that they will be treated with compassion not condemnation, and that they will be offered appropriate help. How do we make that happen?

The late and great copywriter David Abbott (founder of Abbott Mead Vickers, one of the UK's leading advertising agencies), was a great believer in the power of demonstration. He used to say:

> If I tell you I have a beautiful daughter, you'll probably think I'm just a biased, doting father. If I show you a photograph, you might think it's been photoshopped. But if you meet her, you'll see for yourself how beautiful she is.

What he was talking about was the difference between saying something and actually proving it. And proving that things have changed is going to be hugely important if this culture change is going to land properly. First, such a change is highly unusual, and people will be disinclined to believe that it is genuine, let alone that it will be permanent. Second, the personal risks are great. As a management team, you will need to prove that you are serious and that there is longevity to your culture changes. Your staff need to see with their own eyes that a problematic history with alcohol will not in any way be held against someone, but instead that they will be praised for recognizing the problem and getting help to overcome it. This means that at least one senior person needs to go public about their personal struggles with alcohol and the rest of the senior leadership team needs to be equally public in their support of their colleague(s). The judgement-free support will provide the reassurance that people will need before they themselves decide to ask for help.

This can't be a 'once and done' thing though. Culture change happens through repetition and reinforcement. That means everyone changing their attitudes and habits around alcohol and work. There is no room for hypocrisy or double standards. You can't expect the staff to accept a new way of doing things if the senior team are not walking the walk. So that means that Board get togethers should be alcohol-free occasions, and so should client entertaining. My suggestion is that you could involve the staff in coming up with new ideas for how to create bonds with each other and with clients that do not involve alcohol. And if people really can't think of any ways of having fun that don't involve alcohol, that suggests that those people are developing a degree of AUD and could do with some help – some compassionate, judgement-free help (because that is the only sort of help that will be on offer in the new culture you are creating).

What help is available for those who need it?

It's time to look at the types of help that there are out there, and what you might want to offer. Many of you reading this will have Employee Assistance Programmes (EAPs) in place, or an in-house Occupational Health Team, and will assume that these organizations will do the right thing by your employees. I'm sorry to have to tell you that they probably won't.

Here are just a few examples of people being failed by the organizations that were supposed to help them.

Case study 1

A police officer in the UK had an extended leave of absence for stress and depression. Alcohol played a huge part in this, but no-one asked her about it, and she didn't volunteer the information. During this period (and we are talking several months), she had just six counselling sessions, paid for by the Police. And as I said, alcohol wasn't discussed. She went back to work, still drinking, and before too long, her mental health was again so poor that she needed a further leave of absence. As she was being signed off, she explained that she knew she was drinking too much and felt that what she really needed was help with her drinking. She didn't get that help. She was given another six counselling sessions with a counsellor who had no training in addiction, and whose advice was this person should 'try to cut back'. Of course, that advice was useless, and it was several years before that police officer was able to find the support she needed. Support that she paid for herself, and in her own time. In her words, she was able to put alcohol behind her 'in spite of the Police, and not because of it'.

Case study 2

Another police officer, this time in Sweden, had a very similar experience, but in her case, her issues with alcohol were known about from the start. Even so, she wasn't offered any specialist help, just a few counselling sessions, again from someone with no training in, or no understanding of, addiction. She told me that when she returned to work, she felt vilified by her senior officers and her colleagues. The stigma was huge, and her drinking got worse, not better. She eventually lost her job and things spiralled out of control for quite a while. She became severely depressed, and it was many years before she got her life back on track. Another example of a good police officer being completely unnecessarily lost to alcohol. Wherever they are in the world, police officers are doing a difficult and stressful job, which is funded by the public purse. It is not good enough for them to be given no education about the role alcohol plays in exacerbating stress, and to be offered no meaningful help when they develop AUD.

Case study 3

Another example is a nurse in the USA, whose drinking really escalated during Covid. She spoke to the Occupational Health team in the hospital, asking for help. That help was not forthcoming – she was told that 'we're in a crisis and now is not the time for self-indulgence'. She quit her job, because she felt that it was better to leave on her own terms than be fired.

In all of these cases, the individual had tried to address the problem on their own, by attending AA meetings, before asking their employer for help. But as I have already discussed, whilst AA is a lifeline for many, it doesn't work for everyone. Really, though, people should not feel that they are on their own. Around the world, state support is very limited, and is generally very degrading. And even if someone is brave enough to raise the problem with their employer, the help they are likely to be offered may be limited, and often delivered by people with no specialist knowledge of alcohol addiction.

I believe that employers have a responsibility to ensure that the external partners that they use are providing high-quality and effective support and treatment options. And critically they must make sure that people have a *choice* about what help they get. One size does not fit all.

Too many EAPs offer a limited number of counselling sessions, delivered by people with no personal experience of AUD, and little or no training in addiction. As we have seen in the case studies, the individuals receiving this counselling are left feeling shamed, and still drinking.

Other EAPs will pay for someone to attend a rehab clinic, usually as an outpatient, but sometimes as an inpatient. However, rehab clinics generally follow the AA-style 12-step programme and/ or the Sinclair method. The latter involves taking a drug called Naltrexone before drinking to reduce the pleasure of alcohol, allowing individuals to regain control over their drinking habits through a gradual reduction in consumption. It can be effective for some individuals with AUD when combined with support and monitoring, but like AA, it focuses very much on the behaviour (i.e., the drinking). For those who are prepared to do some personal development work, it can be far more effective to help them identify the reasons why they are drinking and reframe those thoughts and beliefs – this is the methodology used by *This Naked Mind* and their growing army of certified coaches. I am obviously biased because I am one of those coaches, but I really do believe that it is important that EAPs offer this type of coaching as an option. And I have two very good reasons for suggesting this.

The success rates of alcohol addiction treatment programmes are difficult to ascertain, not least because the permanency of sobriety can only really be determined once someone has died (i.e., they remained sober for the rest of their life). It is also dependent on self-reporting, and the shame and stigma around AUD means that there may be a tendency for people to claim to be alcohol free when that isn't wholly true. There is no single source of data comparing the results of the different methodologies, and AA do not collect the data. However, there are a number of studies we can refer to.[30] The methodologies are all different, with different sample sizes and research periods, and therefore we can't draw any real conclusions, but it is nonetheless interesting to note that the most expensive option appears to have the lowest success rate. In fairness, that may be because the people who become in-patients at rehab clinics are those whose addiction is more developed, and therefore harder to turn around, than others who attend as out-patients or who follow other methods. But even so, there is a wide variation in cost-effectiveness. There is good evidence from a large-scale meta-analysis[31] that structured rehab programmes have better and longer-lasting results when they are combined with voluntary attendance at AA meetings for an extended period. However, this analysis was conducted in 2019, when *This Naked Mind* was very much in its infancy, and so the research doesn't include it (see Table 12.1).

Cost of treatment – The cost, and cost-effectiveness, of treatment is an important issue for any employer who is funding it, whether directly or indirectly, through an EAP or insurance scheme. It is in everyone's interests that the treatment succeeds and doesn't have to be paid for more than once. Attending AA meetings is free, and a very high proportion of those who go on to paid-for treatment will have started their journey towards sobriety in AA's rooms – certainly that has been my experience in my private coaching work, and in coaching in group programmes for *This Naked Mind*. I say this not to decry AA, but because it is clear that the AA method doesn't work for everyone. And the 12-step programme which lies at the heart of AA's approach is used in virtually every rehab clinic around the world. So, the question is – if the AA method doesn't

---

[30] www.sciencedirect.com/science/article/abs/pii/0306460380900106; www.sciencedirect.com/science/article/abs/pii/S037687160500116X; www.ncbi.nlm.nih.gov/pmc/articles/PMC2565602/#:~:text=In%20the%20group%20that%20received,interval%2C%201.46%20to%203.20

[31] Cochrane Review of Alcoholics Anonymous and other 12-step programs for alcohol use disorder, Kelly, J.F., Humphreys, K., and Ferri, M., 2019.

resonate with someone when they attend free meetings, is it logical to pay a huge amount for that person to go into a rehab clinic that is based on exactly the same method? Wouldn't it make more sense to at least offer them the alternative of a different approach, particularly if it is much cheaper? Giving people a choice about their treatment gives them agency and skin in the game, increasing their motivation and sense of empowerment.

Table 12.1: Comparison of cost and effectiveness of different AUD treatment methods

Treatment method	% AF or moderating and in control	After what period	Research source	Sample	Typical cost of treatment
AA method inpatient programme	51	12 months	Independent	56 'alcoholics'	£18k–£30k (30 days @ £600–£1k / day)
AA method inpatient programme	56	24 months	Independent	56 'alcoholics'	£18k–£30k (30 days @ £600–£1k / day)
AA method intensive inpatient programme	55	36 months	Independent	103 'alcoholics'	£7.5k–£8.5k (28 days)
AA meetings	n/a	n/a	n/a	n/a	No fee
Sinclair method (Naltrexone)	15% more AF/drinking within guidelines versus placebo	16 weeks	Independent COMBINE study (USA)	1,383	Naltrexone costs generally covered by insurance
This Naked Mind – online group coaching	90	various	TNM internal	2,936 course participants	Up to US$2000 for year-long programme
This Naked Mind – private 1:1 Coaching	n/a, but anecdotally 90–95%	Typically 3–6 months	n/a	n/a	£2k–£4k depending on coach and package

The external partners who supply the treatment options will take the path of least resistance. They will carry on doing what they have always done until you, their client, demand change. It is up to you to communicate to them that you want to ensure that everyone who needs help is offered a choice and that they are in a position to make an informed choice. EAPs and Insurers will respond to demand from you, their customers. If you insist that your staff are offered more compassionate and whole-person approaches to overcoming their AUD, as alternatives to the AA 12-step method, those businesses will offer them. And your staff will find true freedom from alcohol, benefiting your business in countless ways.

Confidentiality

A few years ago, mental health issues were taboo, but that has changed, and in time, the same will apply to AUD too. And the speed of the change will depend on leadership teams and high-profile individuals being open about their own experiences so that people have evidence that the new culture of openness really is safe. But there will be a period of transition, during which it will be important to respect people's right to confidentiality. The rule here is very simple – it should always be up to the individual to decide who they tell about their AUD, and when. Treat an employee's AUD as you would any other physical or mental health condition they are suffering from.

Chapter summary

- It is the responsibility of the Board and senior leadership team to ensure widespread buy-in to the changes that are proposed.

- HR's responsibility is to oversee the implementation of the changes, but they will not be able to do this unless the Board have made it clear that this is a non-negotiable – it *is* happening.

- The wellbeing team (which may just be one or two individuals in smaller organizations) should be quite separate from HR, and employees should know that they can speak to them in complete confidence. Treating alcohol as a wellbeing issue rather than an HR issue will encourage people to come forward.

- It is really important that the business researches the options for different types of help, and that it enables individuals who need the help to make an informed choice about the type of help they would like.

- The business should hold suppliers to account and ask for all sensible and practical options to be offered – too many external partners are offering limited choice and poor-quality provision.

- Anyone who receives help has the right to confidentiality for as long as they want it.

13

Sustain the changes by truly embedding a new culture

In the previous two chapters we have been looking at how to determine exactly what the culture around alcohol is going to be in your organization, and how to make that happen. The final thing I want to address is how to make the changes stick.

The changes need to be implemented business wide

The first thing is to ensure that the changes are happening and being sustained throughout the organization, at every level and in every location. Sometimes big initiatives can be embedded very quickly at Head Office, but if they don't feel relevant, they won't filter through to every branch or warehouse or regional or overseas office. The communication between the centre and the branches needs to be strong, credible, and two-way. Those who are running the branches need to be fully bought-in to the rationale for the changes if they are to set the right tone with those they lead. There should ideally be some face-to-face contact with the central leadership team, and it is also important that the training and education offered to those in non-Head Office locations should be of the same quality as for Head Office. And, of course, the treatment options offered should be the same regardless of seniority or location.

Communication is vital and needs to be planned. I would suggest fixing some dates for physical face-to-face meetings where possible

– town halls, quarterly reviews, where leaders from Head Office go on the road to reinforce the message, and to garner feedback. And then there should be regular written/video/online communication, using whatever channels the organization already uses for internal communication. The messages should not just be about the new ways of doing things but need to demonstrate the results by illustrating improved productivity or profitability, or improved mental wellbeing for the individuals concerned. The best way of achieving this is to follow David Abbott's advice (see Chapter 12) and demonstrate the benefits, telling personal stories.

The environment needs to feel different

Employees need to feel safe talking about their difficulties with alcohol, and this will be a gradual change. The new environment must feel different, and this can be achieved through constant reminders not just of the theory, but of examples of senior people addressing their own issues with alcohol, making changes, and winning support and approval for doing so. Senior leaders telling their stories and sharing the changes that have been made at Board level will be really powerful. For example, you could share that alcohol is no longer served at Board dinners or away days, and how much more productive those occasions are as a result. Senior people talking openly about the benefits they have seen from removing alcohol from the workplace culture (or from their lives altogether) will motivate others. Culture change happens when everyone believes that the new way is better – better for them personally and better for the organization.

Celebrate bravery

We are aiming for a complete turnaround when it comes to beliefs about what impact AUD will have on your career. Currently, people fear that if it is known that they have a problem with alcohol, this will hinder their career progression. So they keep quiet and struggle alone, to the detriment of their physical and mental health and to their ability to perform well at work.

We want people to feel safe asking for help. But more than that, we want them to feel that this will actually be a good career move, that they will win the respect of their colleagues and bosses for overcoming adversity in a responsible and empowered way. When I returned to work after my breast cancer, I was praised for my bravery, and that still happens to this day. But to me, I wasn't brave at all, because I didn't have much of a choice. If I didn't have the treatment, I wasn't going to be long for this world.

People with AUD do have a choice. They can carry on as they are, in a private battle with alcohol, hoping that no one will realize what is going on. Hellish as that can be, it doesn't actually require much bravery to carry on as you are. The really brave thing is to acknowledge the problem and ask for help. That takes guts. And overcoming AUD takes commitment and either willpower or some serious personal development work, neither of which are easy. Does your business need people who have the courage to face up to problems, and who have the commitment and personal strengths to overcome those problems? Of course it does! Every business needs people like that. These are the qualities that should boost careers, not hold them back. So, in your business, think about how you can (with their permission, of course) celebrate people who overcome AUD, and how you can demonstrate that this led to career progression for them. Triumph over (potential) tragedy makes for compelling and inspiring stories.

Chapter summary

- The changes need to be implemented business wide.

- It should feel as though there has been a significant change – for the better – within the business.

- Bravery should be celebrated. By making heroes of those who overcome their vulnerability, get help and change things for themselves, the business will encourage others to come forward. They will also be developing a loyal and motivated workforce and making themselves a very attractive employer.

- Employees should ultimately feel that addressing their problems with alcohol will not jeopardize their career progression but enhance it.

14

In conclusion

Sweeping problems under the carpet doesn't make them go away, it makes people trip over the carpet

In this book I have explained the multiple ways in which you may be bottling up trouble and allowing alcohol to harm your business, reducing productivity, and damaging your ability to attract and retain the best people. I have shared the science of what happens in our bodies when we drink alcohol, and how this inevitably contributes negatively to the mental health of anyone who drinks it. I have explained how our society and our workplace cultures have positively encouraged people to drink alcohol, so it is very unhelpful (and hypocritical) to stigmatize anyone who develops a problem with alcohol. Sweeping problems under the carpet doesn't make them go away, it makes people trip over the carpet. I have also shown you how the alcohol-free or sober-curious movement is growing and suggested that changing workplace cultures around alcohol is inevitable – in a few years' time the idea of bars in offices and the routine expensing of alcohol will seem totally anachronistic and out of date. It really is a matter of 'when' and not 'if'.

In the final third of this book, I have given very practical guidance on how to implement the changes that are needed and stressed the need for this to come from the very top of the organization – leaders need to lead, and break down the stigma around this topic by being open and honest about their own experiences. The key planks of the change are to include alcohol-awareness training within wellbeing and stress management programmes, to empower the wellbeing team to develop alternative ways of bringing people together, and to ensure that HR teams are actively facilitating the necessary changes, particularly when it comes to removing and stigma and judgement. And I have made the case for senior leaders to take ownership of the solutions, particularly for those already suffering from AUD themselves, who can really inspire others by sharing their stories. I have also highlighted how important it is that leadership teams do not leave it to occupational health teams or external partners such as Employee Assistance Programmes to decide what support and treatment options are offered to people with AUD. These people are acting on your behalf, and you should be calling the shots.

Those who ignore this advice, and who ignore the societal changes that are happening, will get left behind. By contrast, those who embrace the need for change will see that empowering their employees and showing genuine compassion for anyone in difficulty will result in a significant competitive advantage. I have a team of great people ready to help you seize this opportunity – visit www.bottlinguptrouble.com to access the interactive Bottling Up Trouble assessment tool, or to discuss how to make the changes that will give you a competitive advantage.

Acknowledgements

I have to start by thanking Annie Grace, whose incredible work has changed countless lives, including mine. And thanks too to Scot Pinyard, former Head Coach at *This Naked Mind*.

There are three people who encouraged me to turn my ideas into a book and helped me overcome the imposter syndrome that comes with writing your first book in your sixties – so big thanks to a trio of wonderful women who have coached me – Fiona Parashar, Wendy MacCallum, and Lorna Wilson. Thanks too to Jackee Holder who, along with Fiona Parashar, runs a fabulous, inspiring, and supportive creative writing group. And thank you to Alison Jones and her team at Practical Inspiration Publishing for making this as easy as possible for a rookie writer.

I am indebted to the professional brains that I picked – lawyers Simon Gregory, Karen Bates, and Dale Darling; psychiatrist Corinne Cabanes; Reverend Anne Heywood and Reverend Nigel Done; medic Professor Charlie Knowles.

I have learned a lot from my fellow alcohol freedom coaches, and particularly from my friend, colleague for ten years and co-coach for retreats, Anna Donaghey, as well as Emma Gilmour, Karen Whiston, the late Lori Cook, Christy Osborne, Maria Fox, and Charlotta Gustavson, who have been very generous with their time.

I will not name all of the clients whose experiences are distilled into this book, nor the people I met and interviewed for the book, but you know who you are, and I am so grateful to you for allowing me to retell your stories (albeit, with some details changed to protect your identities). Thank you all for the trust you have placed in me – I appreciate each and every one of you and feel immense joy to see you blossoming in your alcohol-free lives.

My friends have been incredibly supportive. Special thanks to the utterly inspirational Sally Page, who published her first (*Sunday Times* best-selling) novel when she was 60 and warned me that editing would take much longer than anticipated; to Liz Mackie, who gave me a mug emblazoned with the words 'Strong women will change the world', words which have kept me on task as I waded through complicated research papers; to Ann Willis for decades of loving support and a great deal of wise counsel during some tough times, and for reminding me that I can do hard things; to Jeremy Cowdrey for over 40 years of friendship, so many great discussions and a wonderful writing haven in Cornwall; and to Nicky and Simon Heyworth for endless laughs, a guaranteed warm welcome, and countless delicious meals.

And final thanks go to my family for their unstinting support – my ex-husband, John, for his enthusiasm for this project and several great contacts; my brothers Ben and Tom, and my sister-in-law, Katie; my son-in-law Andy Roberts (so much more than tech support!), my daughter-in-law Lois whose input on the cover of the book was invaluable; and finally to my children, Lucy and Eddie, whose encouragement has been limitless – I am so grateful to you both, and so incredibly proud of the people you have become.

Appendix

The National Institute on Alcohol Abuse and Alcoholism in the USA uses the following questions to assess where an individual is on the Alcohol Use Disorder spectrum. It is based on *The Diagnostic and Statistical Manual of Mental Disorders* (DSM), version 5, which is reproduced, for reference, immediately after this list of questions.

In the past year, have you:

1. Had times when you ended up drinking more, or longer, than you intended?
2. More than once wanted to cut down or stop drinking, or tried to, but couldn't?
3. Spent a lot of time drinking? Or being sick or getting over other after-effects?
4. Wanted a drink so badly you couldn't think of anything else?
5. Found that drinking, or being sick from drinking, often interfered with taking care of your home or family? Or caused job troubles? Or school problems?
6. Continued to drink even though it was causing trouble with your family or friends?
7. Given up or cut back on activities that were important or interesting to you, or gave you pleasure, in order to drink?
8. More than once gotten into situations while or after drinking that increased your chances of getting hurt (such as driving, swimming, using machinery, walking in a dangerous area, or having unsafe sex)?
9. Continued to drink even though it was making you feel depressed or anxious or adding to another health problem? Or after having had a memory blackout?
10. Had to drink much more than you once did to get the effect you want? Or found that your usual number of drinks had much less effect than before?

11. Found that when the effects of alcohol were wearing off, you had withdrawal symptoms such as trouble sleeping, shakiness, restlessness, nausea, sweating, a racing heart, or a seizure? Or sensed things that were not there?

The presence of at least two of these symptoms indicates Alcohol Use Disorder (AUD).

The severity of the AUD is defined as:

- **Mild** – The presence of 2–3 symptoms
- **Moderate** – The presence of 4–5 symptoms
- **Severe** – The presence of 6 or more symptoms

DSM-5 Alcohol Use Disorder (reproduced by permission of the American Psychiatric Association)

A problematic pattern of alcohol use leading to clinically significant impairment or distress, as manifested by at least two of the following, occurring within a 12-month period:

1. **Craving**, or a strong desire or urge to use alcohol.

2. There is a **persistent desire** or unsuccessful efforts to cut down or control alcohol use.

3. Alcohol is often taken in **larger amounts** or over a longer period than was intended.

4. Recurrent alcohol use resulting in a **failure to fulfil** major role obligations at work, school, or home.

5. A **great deal of time** is spent in activities necessary to obtain alcohol, use alcohol, or recover from its effects.

6. Alcohol **use is continued despite** knowledge of having a persistent or recurrent **physical or psychological problem** that is likely to have been caused or exacerbated by alcohol.

7. **Continued alcohol use** despite having persistent or recurrent social or interpersonal problems caused or exacerbated by the effects of alcohol.

8. Important social, occupational, or recreational **activities are given up** or reduced because of alcohol use.

9. **Tolerance**, as defined by either of the following:
   o A need for markedly increased amounts of alcohol to achieve intoxication or desired effect.
   o A markedly diminished effect with continued use of the same amount of alcohol.

10. **Withdrawal**, as manifested by either of the following:
    o The characteristic withdrawal syndrome for alcohol.
    o Alcohol (or a closely related substance) is taken to relieve or avoid withdrawal symptoms.

11. **Recurrent alcohol use** in situations in which it is physically hazardous.

Index

Page numbers in *italics* indicate tables and figures

A quick word from Practical Inspiration Publishing...

We hope you found this book both practical and inspiring – that's what we aim for with every book we publish.

We publish titles on topics ranging from leadership, entrepreneurship, HR and marketing to self-development and wellbeing.

Find details of all our books at: www.practicalinspiration.com

 Did you know...

We can offer discounts on bulk sales of all our titles – ideal if you want to use them for training purposes, corporate giveaways or simply because you feel these ideas deserve to be shared with your network.

We can even produce bespoke versions of our books, for example with your organization's logo and/or a tailored foreword.

To discuss further, contact us on info@practicalinspiration.com.

 **Got an idea for a business book?**

We may be able to help. Find out more about publishing in partnership with us at: bit.ly/PIpublishing.

Follow us on social media...

@PIPTalking

@pip_talking

@practicalinspiration

@piptalking

Practical Inspiration Publishing